ALTA VIA

HIGH LEVEL WALKS
IN
THE DOLOMITES

The distant Tyrol from near the start of AV1

ALTA VIA

HIGH LEVEL WALKS
IN
THE DOLOMITES

by
Martin Collins

Published by Cicerone Press
Harmony Hall, Milnthorpe, Cumbria

© MARTIN COLLINS 1986
ISBN 0 902363 75 1
FIRST PUBLISHED 1986
REPRINTED 1990

This book is dedicated to Diana, without whose patience and
enthusiastic support it would not have been compiled.

Grateful thanks are due to Jill Heslop for her assistance with the
Italian language.

All photographs, maps, profiles and view identifications are by the
author. Illustrations of wild-life etc., are by Diana Footer.

CONTENTS

Introduction

Situated towards the eastern end of the Alps' great curve from the Mediterranean coast through central Europe to the Balkans, the Dolomites region occupies an area of northern Italy as large as Wales.

Until the Great War, the South Tyrol, which embraces the northern Dolomites, was part of the Austro-Hungarian Empire. The Treaty of Versailles gave the South Tyrol to Italy but its population remained German-speaking; differences between Austria and Italy are, to this day, a source of underlying friction in the region. During the bitter fighting of 1914-18, avalanches, mountain weather and difficult terrain added to the burden of hardship endured by Austrian and Italian troops alike. Evidence of the war is still clearly visible in the old tunnels and gun positions, discarded mess tins, boot soles and barbed wire.

The Dolomites' name is thought to derive from that of a French geologist - the Marquis de Dolomieu - who wrote enthusiastically about the special qualities of its rock after visiting the area in 1789. The subsequent development of rock and ice climbing throughout Europe is inextricably linked with the Dolomites, many claiming that steep wall climbing - already in full swing before World War I - was born here with pioneers like Paul Preuss, Hans Dulfer and Angelo Dibona establishing difficult routes on the vertical rock.

First ascents of Cima Grande, Monte Cristallo, the Marmolada Tofana and Langkofel were achieved almost exclusively by continental climbers, though our own John Ball, first president of the Alpine Club, reached the summit of Monte Pelmo in 1857. Artificial climbing followed on, with emerging skills and techniques being applied to the great buttresses and faces of the Western Alps during the 1920's and 30's.

Although the Dolomites' reputation as a playground for 'hard men' is fully justified, these mountains are by no means the domain of the rock climber alone. A dense network of footpaths offers endless scope for exhilarating high-level walks; the renowned 'vie ferrate' (rock routes aided by fixed metal ladders and cables) lead up into many sensational situations, while in winter the region becomes a premier skiing destination for thousands of Europeans.

For the hill walker accustomed to British landscape and weather, the Dolomites present as exciting a contrast as can be imagined. Vast tracts of Britain are occupied by rolling uplands and moors, gentle undulations in the land's surface more often than not clothed in vegetation. Movements in the great ice-sheets which once covered northern Europe, together with thousands of years of erosion by rain, wind and frost, have softened and rounded our hills; even in Scotland where the topography is at its most rugged, mountain summits seldom exceed 1200 metres.

The Dolomites could hardly be more different in character! Of relatively modest height compared with the giants of the Central and Western Alps, their soaring limestone peaks reach, nevertheless, up to 3300 metres. Fairy-tale spires, broad rock plateaux, mountain lakes and plunging, forested valleys provide a uniquely stunning environment through which the experienced mountain traveller may pass. Scenery, sometimes bizarre and other-worldly, is always fascinating, while weather conditions tend to be fine and settled.

At present there are seven long-distance high routes - 'Alte Vie' - comprising stretches of footpath, ancient mule tracks and military roads linked together into itineraries of special appeal to the mountain walker. This guide deals with nos. 1 and 2, generally considered to be the finest ones and showpieces of their kind. They run on a north-to-south axis through the very heart of the Dolomites, connecting Tyrolean Val Pusteria with the fringes of the Venetian plain and passing through a wide variety of landscape and human upland settlements.

The walking itself varies from level strolling to scrambling on rock clipped to fixed metal ropes; from long, ambling ascents in forest to steep traverses on scree or snow. Height is maintained throughout at around 2000-2500 metres, dropping to road passes at regular intervals and reaching 2932 metres (over 9600 feet) on Alta Via 2 - the highest point on either route. Everywhere the terrain underfoot is rough, echoing the nature of the mountains through which the paths pass.

The author hopes that these treks through the Dolomites will yield rewarding experiences and enduring memories for readers able to visit this most extraordinary region.

How To Get There

From northern Europe, Alte Vie 1 and 2 are most directly approached over the Brenner Pass, thence via Vipiteno to Bressanone, or Brunico and Monguelfo to Lago di Braies.

Brunico, mid-way between the starting points of both routes, is chief town of Val Pusteria and an important tourist centre, rich in history and art works. Dobbiaco, farther east, is a very scenic alpine town, surrounded by meadows near the Austro-Italian border. Both are well endowed with tourist accommodation.

Fast and comfortable rail links from the Channel ports cross the Brenner Pass to Bressanone, for Alta Via 2. For Alta Via 1, change at Fortezza (Franzenfeste) for the Brunico-Dobbiaco line and get off at either Monguelfo (Welsberg) or Villabassa (Niederdorf), both equidistant from Valle di Braies. There is a mailbus service to Lago di Braies from the Station.

By road, the Autostrada from Innsbruck over the Brenner Pass (toll) is quickest. Vehicles may be left at Bressanone by private arrangement or at the Lago di Braies Albergo for a modest fee. At the end of your journey through the Dolomites, it is possible to return to the start of both routes by mailbus, with a direct service operating in high season. Alternatives include hiring a taxi, or driving to Belluno or Feltre first, with spare clothes etc. left in the vehicle to look forward to!

Many points along both Alte Vie, including refuges, are accessible from motorable roads, though surfaces can be rough. For walkers preferring to sample stretches of route without the commitment of leaving vehicles parked at the start of the Alta Via, the trail could be reached at such access points and a circular walk undertaken; or a driver could take the vehicle on ahead to the next access point for walkers to be met. Notes in the text and sketch-maps contained in this guide will assist plans to take the walking in instalments.

Drivers please note: few Italian roads have central white lines or other markings (even some motorways!). This has the predictable effect of encouraging anarchy and risk-taking, since no law is apparently contravened by vehicles cutting corners or overtaking on the wrong side of the road! Weekends are particularly busy as people make for the hills and cooler conditions.

Maps and Waymarking

This book contains route guides for Alte Vie nos. 1 and 2, with details of terrain, accommodation and supply points, heights, timings, etc. Each stage is outlined by a sketch-map showing important features and is accompanied by a sectional profile, allowing the reader to see at a glance how much ascent and descent is involved between points on the trail.

Walkers in high, rugged mountain country will, however, need to carry maps for four good reasons. First, as a vital navigational aid should the path be missed or if visibility becomes poor. Second, to allow a sensible escape route to be chosen in emergencies such as sickness or injury. Third, to help in planning lower-level alternative itineraries to avoid high, exposed stretches in bad weather. Fourth, to add pleasure to the journey by enabling the identification of features in the mountain environment - peaks, glaciers, cols, settlements, etc.

There are four principal map series covering Alte Vie nos. 1 and 2:-

Kompass produce a green and blue covered 1:50,000 'Wanderkarte' showing numbered footpaths and refuges in red. Whilst just adequate, they leave a lot to be desired. Alte Vie routings are not up to date, contours are at 100 metre intervals making gradients hard to read, and the maps tear easily at folds. However, they do cover the entire area and could be used for planning in conjunction with this guide. Sheets required are nos. 57, 55 and 77 (Alta Via 1); 56, 59 and 76 (Alta Via 2).

Touring Club Italiano have a series of six 1:50,000 'Carte delle Zone Turistiche d'Italia', three of which relate to Alte Vie 1 and 2. They are beautiful maps, the mountains exquisitely engraved in relief. Unfortunately, only a delicate blue and beige are used for water/glaciers and slopes respectively, all other information, including footpaths, appearing in black. Identifying the Alte Vie routing is almost impossible without reference to other material, but nevertheless a graphic picture of the terrain is provided. Relevant sheets are Val Gardena, Cortina d'Ampezzo and S.Martino di Castrozza.

Tabacco offer a good 1:50,000 series with blue covers. The relief is drawn rather crudely but footpaths are overprinted clearly in red; Alte Vie are further identified by blue triangles and, although not numbered, contours are at 50 metres intervals. (See sheets 1 and 4 for AV1; 9, 2 and 4 for AV2). Tabacco also produce an excellent 1:25,000 map in the same style but finely drawn and containing a wealth of detail. Of the four existing sheets (four more are in preparation), only no.3 (Cortina d'Ampezzo) pertains to Alta Via 1.

By far the most useful maps, in the author's opinion, are those in the red Geografica 'Carta Turistica' series. At 1:25,000 they are invaluable on the trail, with numbered paths and refuges overprinted in red, and Alte Vie routes in red triangles. It is a pity that the beginning and end sections of Alta Via 2 and the end of Alta Via 1 lie outside the series' coverage, but other maps can be used as stop-gaps. Sheets needed are nos. 1 and 3 (Alta Via 1); 5, 6 and 10 (Alta Via 2).

Unlike the reliable British Ordnance Survey, whose maps approach the definitive, Italian map-makers cannot seem to agree on spot-heights and Alte Vie routings, which vary from one series to the next. The latter is more understandable, since amendments are constantly being made and official variants added; happily, other inconsistencies are usually minor!

Various hatchings and broken lines are employed to denote a footpath's difficulty. Often a continuous line indicates a broad, easy track or mountain road, a broken line indicating a normal mountain path over mixed terrain, a dotted line a particularly steep or rough section, and a line of crosses a rock route or 'via ferrata'. However, once again there are discrepancies! Whilst a dotted line may not always prove tricky on the ground, some broken-line stretches can come as a nasty surprise!

In the northern regions of both Alte Vie, we are almost in the Austrian Tyrol and place names, as well as conversation, are in German. To avoid tedious repetition of place names in both languages, this guide uses the Italian version throughout.

Waymarking of Alte Vie 1 and 2 is, on the whole, remarkably thorough. Red and white paint stripes on rocks, trees, buildings, etc. signal the routes themselves and often bear additional information such as the path number, the next 'forcella' or refuge and the time taken to reach it. Alta Via numbers also appear inside a painted triangle.

On clear stretches of trail like broad tracks, and sometimes on less frequented stretches, waymarks might become less frequent, sometimes just a single paint flash. But in these cases the way ahead is usually unequivocal and junctions are invariably marked. Signposts are also erected at important intersections and generally seem to escape vandalism and trophy-hunters!

Numerous other numbered footpaths will be encountered too (by and large corresponding to maps), providing the long-distance and day walker with a marvellous network of routes to choose from.

Most of the maps mentioned can be ordered for you at your local outdoor or book shop. However, good stocks are usually carried by Stanfords Ltd., 12, Long Acre, London WC2; McCarta Ltd., 122, Kings Cross Road, London WC1 9DS; or Hachette Ltd., 1, Regents Place, London W1. Naturally they can be purchased from bookshops and outdoor equipment suppliers in Italy.

Clothing and Equipment

Continentals tend to wear brighter clothing in the mountains than their British counterparts, much of it manufactured from traditional materials and of excellent quality. Near the Tyrol in the north, breeches are *de riguer*, as are red-checked shirts, high-mountain boots and even feathered felt hats! Somehow the vastness of the mountains swallows up a gaudiness that on smaller British hills would appear ostentatious.

Three main factors determine what to take and wear: weather, terrain and overnight accommodation (see relevant introductory chapters). In general terms, the weather can be unpredictable with a tendency towards the fine, terrain is unremittingly high and rugged, and the Alta Via walker will either overnight in refuges and mountain inns or camp.

Sound quality equipment suitable for British summer hill-walking will suffice in the Dolomites during the same season. Naturally, experienced hill-walkers have their own ideas on what gear to use but the following notes will help determine its suitability for a trek on an Alta Via.

Versatile clothing, to cope with potentially big changes in weather and temperature levels, is absolutely essential. Multiple thin layers providing flexible degrees of insulation would be preferable to bulky sweaters, duvet jackets and heavy breeches. However, the *total* warmth and protection of clothing should be carefully considered and should be similar to that needed for, say, an extended summer expedition in the Scottish mountains. Snow flurries are quite common on the high Dolomite rock plateaux and there is little shelter.

Shell clothing in the form of cagoule and overtrousers is equally necessary as summer storms can be heavy; rain, wind and low air temperatures at altitude present a real threat if not adequately protected against.

With luck, shorts will be required, as will a lightweight shirt and spare clothing for use in refuges or to change into. Several mountain lakes are passed and the hardier souls amongst us may wish to take a swimming costume in case the weather smiles!

A sun-hat, sun-glasses and high-factor suncream are all indispensable - when the sun does shine, its strength is undiminished in the thin, clear air. Most of the eastern Dolomites are formed from pale rock and, depending on the time of year they are visited, may be partly snow-covered on the higher reaches. The dazzling and burning effects of all this reflected utra-violet radiation can be well imagined.

The ground underfoot is often exceptionally rough - for the most part stones, rock and scree, though there are grassy and forest tracks too: boots and feet can take quite a hammering! Stout footwear that provides adequate ankle support, cushioning and grip on steep slopes is essential. On easier stretches, ordinary 'trainers' might suffice (and are useful in refuges), but they afford insufficient protection on more serious terrain.

Light weight campers should be prepared for pitching high most nights, frequently about 2000 metres (about 6,500 feet). A 2-season sleeping bag will not be much comfort on its own but, combined with a bag-liner or thermal underwear and a closed-cell bed mat, should be warm enough. Hut-hoppers should take a light sleeping bag: blankets are provided, sheets too sometimes, but bivouac hut equipment is less reliable. In any case, a walker who has the ability to bivouac outdoors is always at an advantage in the more remote areas.

A lightweight torch is useful in camp (or refuge) as darkness comes earlier in more southerly latitudes, particularly noticeable late in the season. Mountain peaks can obscure the sun long before it has actually set. Spare batteries and bulb should be carried, as shops are few and far between.

Fuel for cooking is somewhat problematic, again due to the infrequency of shops en route. Camping Gaz in the familiar blue cartridges is available in Italy, but enough for three or four days at least needs to be carried and the route carefully studied for replenishing fuel and other supplies.

Water is not universally abundant in these steep, rocky mountains and backpackers should be prepared on occasions to carry the night's supply until a pitch is found. Indeed, some stretches of trail are completely dry. Having said that, streams and meltwater are encountered and liquid refreshment of all kinds can be obtained from refuges! Water-containers of adequate capacity are clearly important and purifying tablets will provide peace of mind where the source of water is suspect.

A comprehensive first-aid kit is a wise precaution against injury or accident. If it is intended to explore widely off the beaten track, in search, perhaps, of fossils, plants, sighting of wild animals, climbs, etc., a snake-bite kit would be recommended, through the risk of needing to use it is small.

Stout plastic bags are invaluable for keeping rucsac contents dry in rainy weather and for separating clothing, food, documents etc. A map case and compass are useful too, as is a small Italian dictionary or phrase-book.

If a traverse of Forcella della Marmolada on Alta Via 2 is anticipated, involving the ascent of a small glacier, it is advisable to take crampons, ice-axe and rope. Otherwise, it is possible to complete either Alta Via covered by this guide without equipment additional to normal mountain-walking gear, with the following qualifications.

Both routes are for walkers, but it is necessary to add that gradients and exposure are greater in a few places than on most hill walks in Britain. Early in the season, up to about mid-July, an ice-axe is a useful safeguard on late-lying snow on some of the higher north-facing cols. Where metal cables and rungs are fixed to the rock to assist the walker on particularly difficult passages, the following protection technique is recommended by the Club Alpino Italiano.

NOTE: It is important to use karabiners with a large gate to allow clipping onto cables and rungs with large diameters. 'Via ferrata' type protection kits can be obtained from outdoor shops in the Dolomites region.

It will be readily appreciated that by taking along this simple protection kit, scope for off-route exploration on aided paths, rock outcrops and 'vie ferrate' is greatly enhanced for those with a head for heights and used to mountain scrambling or rock climbing.

Terrain, Mountain Safety and Weather

Alte Vie 1 and 2 are of ideal length for the average walking holiday, though precise distances are hard to determine owing to innumerable zig-zags, rough ground and ascents/descents. Alta Via 1 is approximately 120kms (75 miles) long, Alta Via 2 150kms (93 miles).

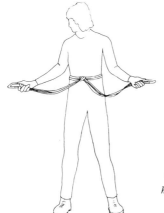

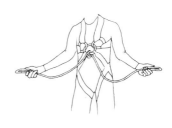

'De-luxe' version - combined sit and chest harness, for extended 'via ferrata' climbing

Long tape sling round waist is tied off leaving 2 loops (50cm/18in), each with large karabiner

Passing a metal cable anchoring peg

Climbing a fixed ladder

Progress along the trail, however, is not always quick and straight-forward and it is best to allow at least ten days for Alta Via 1, up to 2½ weeks for Alta Via 2. Given ideal conditions, very fit walkers could reduce these times considerably, but to hurry through such marvellous country is to miss much. The suggested times allow for the odd excursion off route and episodes of bad weather which can upset the best laid plans.

Alta Via 1 was the first of its kind to be officially established and in many ways remains a showpiece, leading the walker into delectable mountain locations. Only the last stage, from Passo Duran to Belluno, poses any problems - easily by-passed if needs be; elsewhere there are quite lengthy and easy stretches between the higher massifs.

Alta Via 2 is longer and on the whole more rugged in character, climbing and dropping more in total than Alta Via 1 and staying consistently higher. Its final section from Passo Cereda to Feltre is remote, with refuges thin on the ground. For all that, it is an equally fine route, with stunning scenery culminating in the Marmolada - highest peak in the Dolomites.

Because they are renowned and popular with Italians as well as other Europeans, Alte Vie 1 and 2 are well walked by people of all abilities. By no means everyone tackles the routes in their entirety, many preferring to take bites at the most scenic and accessible portions. Indeed, the ability to be walked in stages to suit individual needs is a major attraction of these Alte Vie. Refuges appear at regular intervals (many reached by rough road), thus acting as termini to shorter walks, as well as refreshment and accommodation halts for the long-distance hiker.

Paths themselves are generally well maintained, although they can be damaged and even washed away by exceptionally heavy winter snowfall or rain. Surfaces are frequently as rugged as will be found on any mountain journey in Europe - a mix of stones, rock and scree, occasionally relieved by a rough mountain road or forest track.

Where exposure or steepness exceed normal safe walking limits, artificial protection in the form of metal cable, iron rungs, hoops and ladders is provided; it is not always needed, but is reassuring in wet or icy conditions and if a large pack is carried.

The main exceptions to this adequate level of path safety occur on steep scree just below some *forcellas* (cols), where great care is needed; and on snow or ice patches in north-facing gullies, especially early in the summer, where an ice-axe or staff will balance the walker by acting as a 'third leg'. On such steep snow a good track is invariably trodden in but is subject, of course, to freezing and thawing, either of which increases its difficulty.

Walkers used to British hills should be prepared for substantially more vertical ascent and descent, and greater exposure in places than they are used to. However, paths are often cunningly constructed in zig-zags which takes the sting from many a big climb. Some sections resemble scrambles such as the Snowdon Horseshoe or Helvellyn's Striding Edge and nowhere, except on the descent of the Schiara on Alta Via 1 (avoidable), is the walker expected to have had rock-climbing experience.

For those who have, the Dolomite peaks and walls are peppered with 'vie ferrate', steep and often exposed rock routes which rely extensively on metal cables, rungs and ladders. If you have a good head for heights and a taste for rather more technical expeditions, your rock-climbing experience will be a passport to many sensational ascents and traverses, including some of the major summits if conditions are favourable. (For more information on 'vie ferrate', see *Via Ferrata - Scrambles in the Dolomites* published in this series by Cicerone Press). A simple protection technique used on aided routes is outlined in the section on Clothing and Equipment.

Holiday insurance policies usually cover mountain walking, provided specialist equipment like ice-axe, rope, crampons, skis, etc., are not used. Although Alte Vie are walkers' routes, it would be advisable to check the small print if you intend carrying a protection kit as outlined in this guide.

Hiking in the Dolomites will be enjoyed all the more if your gear is in good condition and you are reasonably fit. Mountain-walking experience is a prerequisite on some sections of both Alte Vie, and a programme of exercising in the month or two prior to departure is recommended if you are not already walking-fit. Such is the nature of the terrain and accessibility, however, that walkers of quite modest ability will find many stretches well within their powers, taking them to unforgettable, high-mountain situations.

Should an accident or illness occur to threaten the walker's life, the international distress call is a series of six visual or audible signals per minute, followed by a minute's pause and then repeated. The reply is three signals per minute, interspersed with a minute's pause. The distress signal can be given in whichever way seems most likely to attract attention: blowing a whistle, shouting, flashing a torch or the sun in a mirror, etc.

Mountain rescue can be initiated from the nearest refuge, many of which are connected to the telephone, but once put into motion cannot be stopped. You are liable for the entire cost of the operation and if a helicopter is deployed, a substantial sum will be incurred, so ensure the decision to summon help is the best or only option!

Such an event is highly improbable for walkers who are properly equipped and provisioned, experienced with map and compass, who keep a weather eye open and are fit enough to deal with the day's planned itinerary.

Weather in the Dolomites is generally drier than that in the Alps farther west and north and there is a tendency towards long, clear, dry spells with calm winds and low average humidity. Certainly the weather is, as a rule, less volatile then Britain's. However, when an unstable air mass associated with changeable conditions moves into the region, periods of rain and low cloud can persist; even when these clear, afternoon thunderstorms can become a regular and predictable feature. Cumulonimbus clouds with great vertical development can be observed building during the morning and early afternoon, so care should be taken to be clear of peaks, ridges and fixed ironmongery, all prone to lightning strike, by the time the storms break. Often the late evening reverts to fine conditions.

Weather in the south of the region is more subject to the effect of damp winds from the plain rising over the Dolomites' southern slopes and causing greater precipitation: this is particularly pronounced in the Feltrini Dolomites on Alta Via 2.

Friday's edition of *La Repubblica* prints weather maps and satellite pictures covering the weekend outlook. Most other daily newpapers carry some kind of forecast, though once on an Alta Via, refuges are the most likely source of information.

Maximum temperatures lie around the mid-70's during May to September, with minima around 50F (lower at higher altitudes). It is less warm in late August and September but, given the choice, this is probably the best time to visit the Dolomites in an average year. Late-lying snow has long since melted and the area often enjoys quiet, clear weather before the nights draw in and the first snows dust the highest peaks in October. During the winter, the Dolomites become a premier skiing location. (Make sure to note closing dates of refuges if you are planning an early-autumn visit).

Even in mid-summer, air temperatures can be low on stretches of both routes, due to their relatively high overall altitude. Cool conditions can be accentuated by wind-chill and it is not unknown for snow flurries to occur. Contrasts, however, can be great, with the chances of finding sunshine and clear visibility greater than in many of Europe's other mountain ranges.

Accommodation, Supplies and Services

Maybe it reflects the relative prosperity of continental walkers, but by far the majority of them stay overnight in refuges (*rifugio*) or mountain inns (*albergo*). As will be seen from their individual specifications in this guide, refuges vary considerably in size and sophistication. Club Alpino Italiano owns and runs a good proportion of them, but private enterprise is represented too. They all serve food and drink (at a price!) and will provide a bed for as few as ten people or as many as a hundred, depending upon their capacity and situation. Some offer catering and facilities of a high standard, others are more basic and many are accessible by 4-wheel drive vehicles.

During the high season (mid-July to mid-August), advance reservations are necessary and cancellations should be notified too, so that vacancies may be filled. Most refuges have a telephone number for bookings (usually, though not always, the refuge itself), and attempts will be made to converse in English; an Italian phrase book is, nevertheless, useful! Some walkers turn up with no prior booking: provided you are early, there is some chance you will be accommodated. By joining the Club Alpino Italiano (apply to C.A.I., Via Ugo Foscolo 3, MILANO - tel: 010-39-2-802-554) a reduction in C.A.I.-owned refuge fees is available.

Not every refuge will launder sheets daily, so a light sleeping bag or liner should be carried, along with a pair of lightweight plimsolls or similar to wear around the sleeping quarters.

A variety of sustaining food is served, such as thick soups, pasta, eggs and potatoes, with omelette and marmalade a popular dessert! Italian beers are weaker than French. Coffee comes strong and black in small cups (*caffè*), frothy in ordinary cups (*espresso*) and sprinkled with powdered chocolate (*cappuccino*).

Collecting individual refuges' rubber stamp impressions, for example in the back of the guidebook, is entertaining: a full tally presented to the Tourist Offices at Belluno (for Alta Via 1) or Feltre (for Alta Via 2) will be greeted with congratulatory noises and a commemorative badge!

Other establishments encountered along the way include *capannas* (huts), bars and *ristorantes* (restaurants). Cable-cars, of which there are several on-route, add their complement of day walkers and trippers to the peaks and plateaux they service: this cuts both ways, since through-walkers can, in turn, gain access to pass or valley for provisioning if required.

With such a generous scattering of refuges along most of both Alte Vie, perhaps it is hardly surprising that backpackers are in a minority. Lightweight camping is not as popular amongst continental long-distance walkers as amongst the British; indeed, it is not permitted at all at some locations on Alte Vie 1 and 2, though this is to discourage casual camping by car-borne tourists rather than the overnight backpacker. Even some refuges are unsympathetic to campers, resenting, perhaps, the loss in revenue.

Backpacking the routes is, however, quite feasible, if occasionally problematic on water-less stretches and steep, rocky ground. Alte Vie 1 and 2 descend when they do to high road passes rather than valleys and towns, so refuges become substitutes for settlements. Whilst meals and drinks can be bought to eke out supplies being carried, re-stocking of basic groceries and hardware usually entails a considerable detour off-route to the nearest town. This can be achieved by using buses (often quite regular) or hitching lifts, but would need to be allowed for in terms of time and cost. Apart from in the terminal towns no banks are passed, so adequate cash should be carried. (Cortina d'Ampezzo off Alta Via 1, and San Martino di Castrozza off Alta Via 2, both contain all supplies and services.)

The real advantages of backpacking, as ever, are its cheapness and the great sense of independence it bestows upon the walker. Freedom from the constraints of crowded accommodation in high season is reward enough for those willing to carry the extra weight! Campsites are only found at much lower levels and are therefore unlikely to be used, unless the walking is to be broken into stages by the use of car or bus services.

Finally there are the permanent, unsupervised bivouac huts (*bivacco*), sited in high or out-of-the-way places to provide shelter for those on extended climbs or walks. Two such huts are passed on each of the Alte Vie covered by this guide. Of metal or more traditional construction (those at lower levels may be a deserted farm building), they are by nature small, rudimentary and only as clean as the previous occupants! Bunks and basic kitchen space will be found, but you will need to be self-sufficient in food, fuel and sleeping gear. Just how welcome a bivouac hut is will depend upon the time of day, weather conditions and your state of exhaustion! In any case, guard against fire and remember to close the door when you leave!

Visitors will find Italy an hospitable country and mountain refuges extend this welcome right up to the high paths used by walkers on Alte Vie 1 and 2. Prices in Italy generally are at present comparable to those in Britain and notably cheaper than in adjacent European countries, though charges for food, drinks and accommodation in refuges reflect transport and maintenance costs.

General tourist information may be obtained from the Italian State Tourist Office, 1, Princes Street, London W1, tel: 01-408-1254.

Geology, Flora and Fauna

A detailed account of the geological structure and evolution of the Dolomites lies outside the scope of this guide. It is possible, however, to sketch a very broad picture of the development to help the walker appreciate some of the processes and natural forces which have shaped these extraordinary mountains.

The Dolomites lie on a base of crystalline schiste and readily eroded layers whose origins are in the depths of ancient seas. Various deposits were subsequently laid down on this base, including sandstone, loam and chalk, into which most of the Dolomite valleys have excavated their courses.

During early geological periods, the whole region was submerged beneath a coral sea, much like those that exist today. Coral reefs and other accumulations of marine organisms eventually formed the massive limestone structures with no obvious stratification which are particularly prevalent in the western Dolomites: the Putia, Odle, Sella and Pale groups and even more compact mountains like the Marmolada.

In later periods (Jurassic and Cretaceous), many friable forms of grey limestone, pink ammonite limestone and loam were laid down, found mainly in the Puez and Vette Feltrine groups.

Following the formation of these great marine deposits, the seabed began to rise as titanic forces shifted and convulsed the earth's crust. In some places the rock strata broke up, in others becoming folded and overlapped, reversing the original positions of the layers. Over the millions of years it takes for geological changes to occur, upheaval following upheaval, the exisiting conformation of the Dolomites was reached.

21

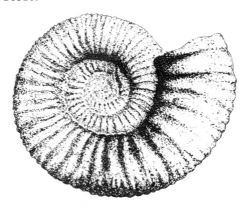

Ammonite fossil

By contrast, the effect of glaciation and erosion by frost, rain and wind are relatively fast-moving. Progressive landslides and the inexorable flaking of rock walls are clear for the walker on either Alta Via to see: in places, the routes have been redirected round landslips and associated debris.

The story of living organisms that populated these sedimentary and cretaceous rocks, before they were elevated into mountain form, is told in myriad fossil remains. These imprints of creatures and plants, shells and corals, are spread through various layers and the observant traveller will spot many examples - particularly on the limestone tablelands of Puez and Pale di San Martino.

Perhaps more than any other Alpine region, the Dolomites are richly abundant in flora, from olive trees on the northern fringes of the Venetian plain to rock-loving saxifrage and bellflowers up to a height of 2500m.

Between valley bottoms and the bare, rocky heights exists a profusion of trees, bushes and undergrowth, with species too numerous to catalogue here; among them are found rhododendrons, whortleberries, hazelnuts, wild cherries and raspberries, juniper, ferns and, less commonly, orchids and lilies.

Wild flowers add brilliant colour to meadow, alp and high path alike, including such species as the Rhaetian Poppy, Purple Saxifrage, Spotted Gentian, Devil's Claw, Pink Cinquefoil, Dwarf Alpenrose and Edelweiss.

It is always with a sense of wonder and incredulity that one comes across flowers on barren rocky slopes above 2500m, but even here, brightly coloured species thrive in cracks and crannies. Amongst these true alpines, the jewels of high mountain locations, are the brilliant blue stars of the Spring Gentian, the delicate purple Alpine Pansy and the bright pink flower-cushions of Rock Jasmine.

Regrettably, picking wild flowers is a common practise in Italy, as elsewhere in mountain Europe. Once-common plants like edelweiss are becoming harder to find and one wonders how long it will be before the rarer species disappear altogether in more popular areas. With so many visitors using the mountain environment for sporting and leisure activities, conservation of natural habitats should be uppermost in all our minds.

Because both Alte Vie routes take the walker through far more high alpine terrain than valley or lowland, the range of fauna likely to be encountered is quite narrow during the summer season. There are,

Edelweiss

Marmot

naturally, many species of birds, mammals and insects living in diverse habitats which are common to Britain too. However, the creatures most likely to interest the Dolomite high-level walker are those whose very presence epitomises wild mountain country.

Commonest by far is the marmot, a cuddly, beaver-like animal up to 60cms (2 feet) in length which hibernates from mid-October to mid-April. Although worldwide there are some 13 species, it is found in its original habitat only in the Alps and High Tatras, its wolf-whistle warning cry heard on grassy and stony slopes up to about 2700m. Marmots live gregariously in burrows reached down 3 metres and as much as 10 metres in length, with several exits. Each individual weighs about 5 to 6 kgs, living off plant greenery and, during hibernation, body fat. In late May or early June, females give birth to up to six naked and blind young.

Another exciting high-mountain mammal to observe is chamois, though shyness makes it more elusive. These animals can sometimes be spotted on precipitous rocky slopes, over which they move with uncanny agility, living in groups of between 15 and 30 individuals.

Other creatures which may, with good fortune and patience, be glimpsed in the forests include stags and roe-deer, squirrels and the capercaillie, a wood-grouse much prized as a game bird. On the high rock plateaux, alpine hares and even the occasional Golden eagle might be seen. Adders are common today in much of the Alps, so care should be taken to avoid being bitten if one is encountered at close quarters.

Other bird species are represented - white partridge, mountain pheasant, imperial raven, jackdaw and alpine chaffinch - but an Italian penchant for hunting has decimated many of these wild creatures. It is encouraging to note, however, the establishment of Nature Parks in which they are now protected: the Paneveggio/Pale di San Martino Park, and Piazza del Diavolo in the Feltrini Alps on Alta Via 2 are good examples. It is hoped to link all these separate reserves into a future Dolomites National Park.

Photography

Passing so much unusual topography on both Alte Vie, the prospects for photography are exceptionally interesting. Rock formations are varied, frequently dramatic, with dizzy views a feature from many stretches of path.

Surpassing all else, however, is the quality of light, especially in fine weather. Sunrise and sunset are the two most magical moments of the day, when the upper crags and summits are lit yellow, golden and deep red by the low sun - an unforgettable visual experience. At other times, there is a dazzling brilliance of sunshine on rock and snow, while at lower altitudes farmsteads, barns and settlements add human interest. Even in changeable weather, rain and mist invariably give way to dramatic clearances.

Pocket cameras producing a small negative (such as sizes 110, 126 or disc film) are likely to yield disappointing results unless the subject is at close range: useful in and around refuges, especially with integral flash, but no competition for the larger 35mm format cameras when it comes to views. A good compromise is the 35mm compact, small enough for shirt or rucsac pocket and capable of taking good pictures. A compact has the added advantage of easy operation on awkward sections of path or on *vie ferrate*.

More serious photographers will take along at least one camera body and a couple of lenses to vary the perspectives and impact of their shots. Zooms, though heavier than prime lenses, are more versatile on steep, rough ground.

Useful filters with colour film are a polarizer for darkening blue skies and reducing reflections on water or glass: a UV or skylight filter for general use; and a ½-stop pale-brown filter to neutralise excessive bluish casts at high altitude. For black and white film, a yellow-green filter enhances skin tones outdoors, lends a little modelling to snow and establishes lively skies. An orange or red filter will dramatically cut haze from distant views.

Exposure can be tricky in dazzling sunshine surrounded by pale rock and snow. The only sure guarantee of good results is to bracket widely, exposing a stop or more (in ½-stop intervals) either side of the estimated correct setting.

Camera equipment is vulnerable to moisture, dust, impact and heat - all encountered on the trail each day! Padded pouches are commercially available which attach to a rucsac hip-belt or will tuck into a rucsac pocket: without such protection, a camera dropped on typical Dolomite ground is unlikely to survive!

It is advisable to take film stock with you; although it can be purchased en route, storage conditions are often far from ideal. Heat is film's number one enemy and can significantly degrade the quality of the processed image, particularly colour. Unused and exposed film stock can be packed deep within the rucsac, surrounded by insulating items like spare clothing and sleeping bag. To avoid possible X-ray damage if posted back to Britain for processing - not to mention the vagaries of the European postal service - film is probably best carried home with you!

Explanation of Route Guides

In order to split both routes into manageable chunks, Alta Via 1 appears in three sections, Alta Via 2 in four. Each section represents approximately three days of walking, taking into account stops for meals, photography, off-route detours and occasional bad weather. Each section also starts and ends at a town or major road pass, giving scope for breaking the walk to obtain supplies or to be picked up by car.

The principal official variants are outlined in the text in smaller type and are drawn on the sketch-maps too, facilitating a choice of alternative routings should circumstances dictate. The stages in this guide, however, are suggestions only and individual walkers may well develop different objectives to suit their own pace and available time.

Important landmarks along the trail, such as refuges, *forcellas*(cols), road passes, path junctions, etc., are printed in heavy type and are preceded by the time it takes to reach them from the previous landmark. (Timings are based on a moderately laden walker's steady pace and do not include prolonged stops). Heights above sea level, in brackets, are expressed in metres but a conversion table appears at the back of this book.

The locations, owners, capacities, opening periods, accessibility and telephone numbers of refuges along the way are included, as are occasional references to possible camping pitches and car parking space near the path. (N.B: Refuge opening/closing dates are subject to amendment if snow or weather conditions are exceptional. If travelling very early or late in the season, check first).

Readers will find sectional profiles accompanying each stage of the walks, showing what ascent/descent is involved en route. Thus by studying this guide and assessing what terrain and amenities lie ahead, it is possible for individual walkers, whatever their style of travel, to plan each day's objectives with confidence.

Route directions throughout are given for the south-bound walker and in the text are abbreviated thus: R = right, L = left. Compass points are also expressed as initial letters, e.g. NE = north-east, S = south, etc. Alta Via 1 and 2 appear as AV1 and AV2.

A short glossary has been included, giving translations of words the mountain walker is likely to find useful. There is also a table to convert heights above sea-level, which are given throughout in metres, to feet.

Changes to Alta Via routings and their variants do occur from time to time, as do the specifications of refuges. However, to the best of the author's knowledge, all the information contained in this guide is accurate at the time of going to press.

KEY TO MAPS

▬ ▬ ▬ ▬ ▬   ALTA VIA

⌐ ⌐ ⌐ ⌐   OFFICIAL VARIANT

○   TOWN

⬠   REFUGE ON MAIN ROUTE

⬟   REFUGE OFF MAIN ROUTE

■   BIVOUAC HUT

▪   MOUNTAIN FARM

〜〜〜   ROAD

▲   MOUNTAIN SUMMIT

◈   LAKE

⊤⊤⊤⊤⊤⊤⊤⊤   CABLE-CAR OR CHAIR-LIFT

'King of the Alps'
(Dwarf Forget-Me-Not)

ROUTE GUIDE

ALTA VIA 1

*Monte Cristallo (3221m) and its outliers
from Rifugio Lagazuoi*

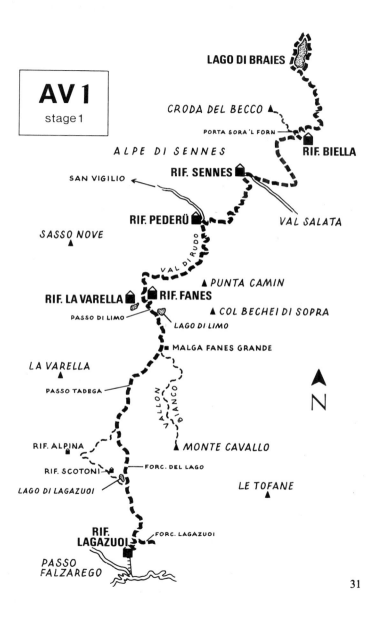

LAGO DI BRAIES

CRODA DEL BECCO ▲

PORTA SORA 'L FORN

RIF. BIELLA

ALPE DI SENNES

RIF. SENNES

SAN VIGILIO ←

VAL SALATA

RIF. PEDERÜ

SASSO NOVE ▲

VAL DI RUDO

▲ PUNTA CAMIN

RIF. LA VARELLA   RIF. FANES

PASSO DI LIMO

▲ COL BECHEI DI SOPRA

LAGO DI LIMO

■ MALGA FANES GRANDE

LA VARELLA ▲

PASSO TADEGA

VALLON BIANCO

▲ MONTE CAVALLO

RIF. ALPINA

RIF. SCOTONI

FORC. DEL LAGO

LAGO DI LAGAZUOI

LE TOFANE ▲

RIF. LAGAZUOI

FORC. LAGAZUOI

PASSO FALZAREGO

STAGE 1:
Lago di Braies to Rifugio Lagazuoi

From lovely Lago di Braies, Alta Via 1 ascends through forest and a
rocky valley to its first pass under the rock peak of Croda del Becco,
with outstanding views ahead. On good tracks past patches of forest,
lakes and mountain farmsteads, and taking in several refuges, height
is gradually gained as the route penetrates higher mountain terrain. A
steep forcella is crossed to another lake and we approach a rugged area
of cliffs and rock towers rich in relics from the conflict between Italian
and Austrian troops in World War 1. At 2752m, Rifugio Lagazuoi is
the highest point reached so far, perched at the top of a cable-car from
Passo Falzarego and providing sensational panoramas over this region
of the Dolomites.

* * *

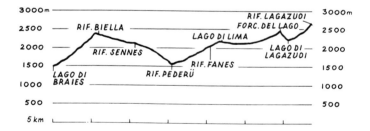

AV1 is waymarked from the hamlet of Schmieden, 3kms down the picturesque Valle di Braies, but the start is generally accepted to be the beautiful lake known as Lago di Braies. The valley itself contains only one shop, other buildings being dwellings, restaurants and hotels, so provisions for the first part of the walk need to be carried in, particularly if you are backpacking. There are shops at Monguelfo and at Villabassa in Val Pusteria.

At first, the valley approaches are dominated by the rock spire of Sasso del Signore (2447m) and its buttresses to the E, but before long the southern horizon is filled by the great north face of Croda del Becco soaring above pine forest to 2810m.

LAGO DI BRAIES (1500m) - *a very popular holiday and weekend destination for Italian families, and justly so. Its turquoise waters are fringed with little white shingle beaches and encircled by a good, much-walked track. Not surprisingly, there is ample car parking space, boating on the lake, a large alpine-style hotel (Albergo Lago di Braies, open 30th May*

Lago di Braies 33

to 25th Sept.), souvenir shops and a bar/restaurant. Camping, however, is barred - understandably considering the location's natural qualities and the heavy use it receives. Several buses a day run up to here from the railway station at Villabassa.

Take the path past a chapel, undulating pleasantly along the lake's west shore through pine forest. At the S end, leave the shoreline path at a prominent waymark and climb through low conifers in steady zig-zags to a

1 hr - **PATH JUNCTION** - The L branch continues to climb in forest, crosses a small cliff and mounts a bluff to emerge at

20 mins - **TOP OF A RAVINE & SIGNPOST** - (An alternative and shorter route to here from the path junction takes the R branch, crosses a stream bed and attacks the steeper slopes in the ravine itself, nowhere difficult.)

From the signpost, take a path R, still steep but well made,

Walkers at Porta Sora'l Forn.
Monte Cristallo top left   Monte Pelmo top right

following waymarks up and out of trees, with marvellous views E to glaciated peaks in the distant Tyrol.

A rising traverse over scree and a short rocky passage equipped with steel cable (the first of several aided sections we shall encounter, but here quite superfluous except in wet or icy conditions) leads up to a

40 min - **SIGNPOST** - Turn R, at first on the level (possible wild camping if water carried), beneath the high, striated cliffs of Monte Muro L, heading up a rocky valley on zig-zags to emerge at

45 min - **PORTA SORA 'L FORN** (2388m) - *The view in clear weather is immense and amply rewards the relentless climb from Lago di Braies. To the SW glitters the Marmolada's glacier, in the S rises the wedge of M.Pelmo, to the SE Monte Cristallo - profiles which will become familiar companions on our journey S.*

(From the crucifix on the pass, an entertaining path zig-zags cleverly NW (in about 1 hr 15 mins) up a steep corner of mountain to the summit of Croda del Becco (2810m): the panorama from this elevated spot is quite breath-taking.)

Rifugio Biella from Porta Sora'l Forn
Cloud-capped Monte Pelmo distant right

35

Below to the L stands

10 min - **RIFUGIO BIELLA** - (2300m) - *CAI Treviso section; 40 places; open 1/7 to 15/9; tel. 0474/75119.*

AV1 now follows the jeep track (path 6) W then SE round a large depression in the Alpe di Sennes, turning sharply W round Col di Siores and dropping to join a track from Val Salata, before reaching the pleasantly situated

45 min - **RIFUGIO SENNES** (2116m) - *Privately owned; 45 places; open mid-June to end-Sept; tel. 0474/51092.*

Leave the refuge with its small lake, SE on path 7, still on the jeep track (once an old military road). The way crosses the flowery Pian di Lasta, ignoring a L turn to Rifugio Fodara Vedla, and zig-zags down between Colle della Macchina to the N and Colle di Rü to the S. Descending more steeply, the track, now in patchy forest, reaches a gully and arrives at

1 hr - **RIFUGIO PEDERÜ** (1548m) - *Privately owned; 25 places; open mid-June to end-Sept; tel. 1474/51086. Connected NW to San Vigilio di Marebbe in Val Badia by a motorable road.*

A rough mountain road now climbs S with numerous hairpins up Vallone di Rudo, passes Lago Piciodèl in its wild rocky environment, to reach trees and

1½-2 hrs - **RIFUGIO FANES** (2060m) - *Privately owned; 65 places, open 15/6 to 15/10; tel. 0474/51097.*

The refuge is decorated with wartime relics, including large shell-cases on the balcony. About 15 min W from the main route stands

RIFUGIO LA VARELLA (2042m) - *Privately owned; 40 places; open mid-June to end-Sept; tel. 0474/51079.*

A jeep will take up to 6 passengers at a time (and at a price!) from Rifugio Pederü to Rifugio Fanes or La Varella, much to the disdain of walkers whom it passes and covers in dust!

High peaks surround us: above Rifugio La Varella and tiny Lago Verde rises the Pices Fanes dome with Sasso delle Dieci and Sasso delle Nove; to the SW, Cima Paron and La Varella; to the E, Col Bechei di Sopra and to the NE Punta Camin.

Climbing SE, the rough track soon reaches Passo di Limo (2172m) and the popular day-trip destination of Lago di Limo, thereafter dropping S to

36

1 hr - **MALGA FANES GRANDE** (2104m) - Shortly after leaving the mountain road R at a hairpin, a junction is reached where the track crosses a marshy depression.

(The L fork, path 17, is a variant going SE then S up Vallon Bianco to the summit of Monte Castello and along the ridge to Monte Cavallo (2912m). The ridge was intensively fortified during World War 1 and still bears the remains of timbered trenches, tunnels and artificial pathways clinging precariously to the shattered rock. Despite these attractions, the ascent is rough and the descent into Val Travenanzes dangerously steep: the traverse is not an easy one! This variant rejoins the main route near Forcella Col dei Bos).

AV1 (path 11) keeps to the mule track, ascending gently to Passo Tadéga (2153m). Just before the pass, a trod branches R to climb to the summits of La Varella (3055m) and Cunturines (3064m).

Ahead, over clumps of trees, rears the wedge-shaped Cima del Lago, with the Forcella del Lago through which we pass a conspicuous notch to its L.

Forking L at Col Locia, the rough eastern flanks of Val di Fanes are climbed due S, with screes leading more steeply up to the impressive

1 hr 45 min - **FORCELLA DEL LAGO** (2486m).

NOTE: The descent S from this forcella, over loose scree and rock, is very steep and is best attempted by those with a steady head for heights who can move securely on difficult ground. A longer but easier alternative lies in taking the R path fork at Col Locia, up over Forcella Col Locia round the NW corner of Cima del Lago. This path (no.11) drops W (ignore a path climbing S) through patchy forest to a jeep track above Rifugio Alpina (1726m). Here, turn sharp L (SE) up the Vallon di Lagazuoi on track 20, past Rifugio Scotoni (1985m) to meet the main route at Lago di Lagazuoi. Allow an extra hour for the detour.

Descending from Forcella del Lago, the scree path joins a well defined and waymarked track (no.20) above the attractive Lago di Lagazuoi. Taking the R fork, climb gradually almost due S across the Alpe di Lagazuoi over rocky terrain, with the great line of cliffs on Lagazuoi Grande ahead L.

At a yellow signpost, AV1 makes a bee-line for the refuge, visible (in clear conditions!) on the ridge ahead. Shaley slopes have been bulldozed for winter skiiers and the 200m climb is an uninspiring trudge. Once again however, and this is so often the case in the Dolomites, effort is rewarded!

1 hr 45 min - **RIFUGIO MONTE LAGAZUOI** (2752m) - *Privately*

Forcella del Lago from the south

owned; 12 places; open all year; tel. 0436/5991.

This is the highest point reached so far and given good weather the views are unforgettable, with range upon range of mountains laid out like a map in all directions. There is food and drink too, and a cable-car ride down to Passo Falzarego for more of the same, with the added bonus, if required, of public transport right down to the fleshpots of Cortina d'Ampezzo (all supplies and services). However, the descent is a long one and steps must be retraced....

The refuge may be by-passed if time or weather press, or if its attractions aren't sufficient to justify the climb up! In this case, keep L above a marshy depression and climb SE to the Forcella Lagazuoi (2571m).

Alpenrose

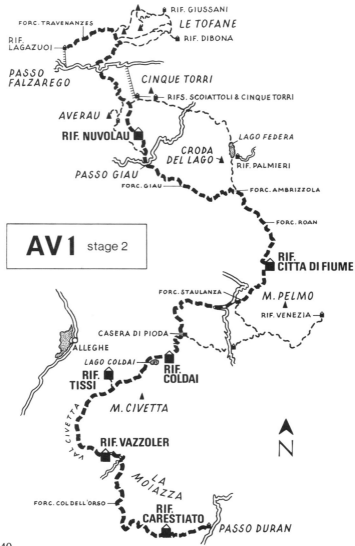

FORC. TRAVENANZES

RIF. GIUSSANI

RIF. LAGAZUOI

LE TOFANE

RIF. DIBONA

PASSO FALZAREGO

CINQUE TORRI

RIFS. SCOIATTOLI & CINQUE TORRI

AVERAU

RIF. NUVOLAU

LAGO FEDERA

CRODA DEL LAGO

RIF. PALMIERI

PASSO GIAU

FORC. GIAU

FORC. AMBRIZZOLA

FORC. ROAN

AV1 stage 2

RIF. CITTA DI FIUME

FORC. STAULANZA

M. PELMO

RIF. VENEZIA

CASERA DI PIODA

ALLEGHE

LAGO COLDAI

RIF. TISSI

RIF. COLDAI

M. CIVETTA

RIF. VAZZOLER

VAL CIVETTA

LA MOIAZZA

FORC. COL DELL'ORSO

RIF. CARESTIATO

PASSO DURAN

N

40

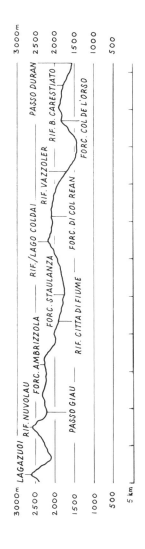

41

STAGE 2:
Rifugio Lagazuoi to Passo Duran

From World War I galleries hewn into the Lagazuoi and Castelletto mountains, close to the great summits of Le Tofane above bustling Cortina d'Ampezzo, Alta Via 1 climbs to the Nuvolao. This rocky peak with its popular refuge is one of the finest panoramic viewpoints in the entire Dolomite range. A steep descent leads to grassier hillsides and a succession of passes in easy, mixed terrain beneath the imposing bulk of Monte Pelmo. Rough mountain roads lead to a high farm and the ascent to Rifugio Coldai, a good base for experienced climbers keen to reach the summit of Monte Civetta. In sensational mountain scenery under the Civetta's 7km-long west face, we leave the delightful Lago Coldai, drop down flowery Val Civetta and cross lower cols, in and out of forest. Three refuges are passed before the trail arrives at pastureland around Passo Duran.

* * *

Chamois

Caves and scattered timbers on the slopes of Lagazuoi Grande date from World War I, when this area was given over to fighting between Austrian and Italian troops. Old fortifications abound and Italy's present-day armed forces, complete with artillery mule-trains, still use the area for exercises. The sight and sounds of smoke-bombs, gunfire, hovering helicopters, jet aircraft on mock bombing runs and convoys of armed troops is likely to alarm the unsuspecting visitor, but the Italian tourists themselves seem to take it in their stride! Perhaps they are more accustomed to the Latin way of doing things than us northern Europeans!

The rock towers of Lagazuoi Grande
from the head of Val Travenanzes

43

In fact, the crest of Piccolo Lagazuoi beneath the refuge contains a labyrinth of underground wartime passages. During World War I, the main summit was held by Austrian troops whose attempts to dislodge the Italians from the Martini ridge half way down the south wall, using powerful mines, produced scars on the mountainside which are clearly visible today.

In turn, the Italians took the east summit with a similar operation and their munitions gallery *('Galleria Lagazuoi')* has been renovated for visitors to look round. A torch is necessary (can be hired at refuge) and a path leads down into the gallery, emerging at Passo Falzarego in about one hour. From the road pass, Forcella Lagazuoi may be reached on foot up a plain path, or the cable-car taken back to Rifugio Lagazuoi.

From Forcella Lagazuoi, take path 402 down to Forcella Travenanzes (2507m) - not the obvious path dropping directly to Passo Falzarego, as AV1 is shown on some maps. The maze of trods and

The Tofane Massif

44   *Monte Castelletto's separate summit just above the figure*

tracks in the vicinity bears witness to its popularity, but keep ahead NE (wild pitches near streams) and turn R at a waymarked boulder, still on path 402.

Val Travenanzes stretches away to the L, an immensely rugged place, littered with boulders and shattered rock and bounded to the W by the screes and rock towers of Lagazuoi Grande, to the E by the Tofane massif.

Near the path stands a World War I memorial stone, surrounded by rusty barbed-wire, shell cases and old boot soles - startlingly graphic reminders of the bitter fighting which took place here around 70 years ago. A little farther on are the remains of buildings and slit trenches. Walking S, we soon reach

30 min - **FORCELLA COL DEI BOS** (2330m).

(From here, a path beneath the S cliffs of Tofane di Roces leads to the entrance of the *Galleria del Castelletto*. The Castelletto, a SW spur of the Tofane, was held by the Austrians and dominated Italian positions at Col dei Bos and in Val Costeana. As a result, it was the object of repeated and bloody direct attacks until finally, at 3pm on July 11th 1916, the summit was blown up by 35 tons of explosive, causing terrible loss of life amongst the defenders. A further day of hard fighting ensued before Italian Alpine troops were able to claim the shattered summit.

The gallery, suitably repaired for visits, is a moving testimony to those terrible events. A torch will be needed, and a steady head in places.

Climb the small cliff (metal steps and ropes) to gain access to the cave entrance, past remnants of a dug-out hut. The gallery itself zig-zags up inside the mountain, about 6 metres from the cliff face. Wooden steps and handholds are provided where the gradient steepens.

Hollows hewn into the walls at intervals formed sleeping quarters, ammunition stores, gun chambers and latrines; deep grooves in the rock floor were worn in by the movement of artillery. Information boards explain features within the gallery before the route passes the explosion crater and emerges at the cliff face near the top of the Castelletto (2675m). Allow about an hour from Forcella Col dei Bos. To return, take the waymarked ledge and aided path.)

The *Lipella via ferrata* leaves the Castelletto, crossing the great west flank of Tofane di Roces to the summit of Tre Dita (2760m) on a series of metal ladders and rock pitches protected with steel ropes: definitely only for experienced and equipped climbers. There is another World War I position on Tre Dita, and a rocky descent can be made SE to Rifugio Guissani (2561m) near the old Cantore refuge - *(CAI Cortina section; 56 places; open mid-June to mid-Sept; tel. 0436/5740).*

Half-way down to the refuge, the 'normal' ascent route to Tofane di Roces (3225m) branches sharp R, but itself needs climbing experience and possibly ice-axe and crampons. Allow at least 5 hours from Forcella Col dei Bos over to Rifugio Guissani, and an extra 3 hours for an ascent to Tofane di Roces.

A number of rock routes and *vie ferrate* climb the imposing walls of the Tofane group and a cable-car reaches the highest point -Tofane di Mezzo (3245m) - from Cortina d'Ampezzo. There are paths beneath the S wall (nos. 404 and 412), allowing non-climbers access to Rifugio Guissani and Rifugio Dibona, should a more thorough exploration of this interesting mountain be contemplated.

NOTE: many of the high *vie ferrate* routes are snow-bound until after the end of July.

From Forcella Col dei Bos, AV1 drops S, cutting the zig-zags of a broad wartime track and leaving path 402, which heads SE for the valley. Now on 412, pass through a short tunnel and at a junction on a bend, fork R, immediately taking a thin, unwaymarked trod down L. Threading pleasantly through forest, with exciting views of Cinque Torri's rock towers across the valley, we emerge at the Cortina-Passo Falzarego road and

30 min - BAR/RESTAURANT MAGISTRATO ALLE ACQUE (1985m) - *about 2kms below Passo Falzarego.*

Turn L down the road for 200 metres and take path 440, S then E up through forest. Veering S again on zig-zags, the route brings us onto open mountainside under a line of cliffs, swings round E beneath the rocky peak of Averau (2649m) and levels off at a

1 hr 15 min - PATH JUNCTION.

Here, on a grassy alp, the main route and a good variant diverge, reuniting at Forcella Ambrizzola, 4 to 5 hrs distant. The main route there is described first, followed by a summary of the variant.

A short stroll away and easily visited for refreshment is the modern Rifugio Scoiattoli *(privately owned; 15 places; open beginning July to mid Sept; tel. 0436/61939).*

NOTE: A chair-lift runs to Rifugio Scoiattoli from the Cortina-Passo Falzarego road, saving non-purists a 275m climb. To reach it, drop E

Rifugio Nuvolau

down the road from Bar Magistrato for about 1½kms, taking a track off R to Rifugio Bain de Dones, the chair-lift station.

The extraordinary cluster of Cinque Torri's five rock towers soars to the E, all that remains of an ancient turreted mountain. With rock climbs of all grades on their flanks, there is every likelihood of seeing climbers perched high above.

From the path junction near Rifugio Scoiattoli, AV1 turns R (S) over rocky slopes, climbing steadily above low cliffs and follows a well marked and popular route up to

45 min - **RIFUGIO NUVOLAU** (2575m) - *CAI Cortina section; 26 places; open mid-June to end-Sept; tel. 0436/61938.*

(A parallel ascent route to here passes Rifugio Averau (2413m), situated a little W and a good base for climbing the *Averau via ferrata* - about 1 hr each way. A connecting path rejoins AV1. An alternative route ahead to Passo Giau, by-passing steep ground beyond the Nuvolao, leaves SW then SE on path 452.)

The Nuvolao is one of the premier viewpoints in the entire Dolomites region and in clear conditions, panoramas from the rocky crest are of a very special order. Behind us to the N lie the Tofane, Lagazuoi and the now dwarfed Cinque Torri, while to the S minor

Retrospective view from the Nuvolao: Cinque Torri centre,
48   *triple peaks of the Tofane centre top, across Val Costeana*

rock towers and ridges lead the eye to the great wedge of Monte Pelmo.

Proceed SE to the end of the little summit ridge and descend a scrambly rock pitch, surprisingly abrupt and aided by metal cable. An easy, flatter section is followed by a long, scree-filled gully leading down to grassy meadows at

1 hr - **PASSO GIAU** (2236m) - *and Rifugio Passo Giau (privately owned; 36 places; open beginning June to mid-Oct; tel. 0437/ 720130).*

Take path 436 to the L of a small chapel, contouring round grassy slopes with wonderful retrospective views to the Nuvolau refuge, the Tofane and, in the W, the Marmolada and Sella group. At the little Forcella di Zònia, bear R beneath Col Piombin to reach a well defined but un-named.

20 min - **FORCELLA** (2239m).

AV1 drops round E in Val Cernera, dominated ahead by the flat-topped bulk of Monte Formin (2657m), before climbing a small valley to cross

Ra Gusela, centre, the Averau Peak, distant left,
from Passo Giau   49

45 min - **FORCELLA GIAU** (2360m).

Taking the L (SE) path fork and dropping to pass the marshy Lago delle Baste, AV1 follows Monte Formin's impressive S cliffs and crosses several stream beds before rising NE to be joined by 2 other paths coverging on

1 hr 15 min - **FORCELLA AMBRIZZOLA** (2277m).

Variant from Rifugio Scoiattoli: A good track E leads quickly past the Cinque Torri rocks to

20 min - **RIFUGIO CINQUE TORRI** (2137m) - *privately owned; 20 places; open mid-June to end-Sept; tel. 0436/2902.*

A mule track is followed to a bend where we leave E on path 437, descending into forest to cross the Cortina-Passo Falzarego road at Ponte di Rocurto (1708m) and the Rio Costeana stram. Another mountain road is crossed as path 437 climbs up and round in forest, down and out of Val Formin where a good mule track is joined. Climbing more steeply NE, we turn the sharp northern

CAMPANILE
INNERKOFLER

CRODA
DA LAGO

Rifugio Palmieri

spur of Croda del Lago, whereafter the variant veers sharply S and falls gently to the beautiful

2 hrs - LAGO DI FEDÈRA *(2055m) - and Rifugio Gianni Palmieri (CAI Cortina section; 30 places; open beginning July to mid-Sept; tel. 0436/2085).*

Croda del Lago (2701m) rises precipitously to the W, a classic Dolomite mountain with several *campaniles* - sharp spires of rock - and rock-climbing routes, all of which require previous experience.

A jeep track to Cortina d'Ampezzo leaves from the refuge near the lake's S end. Take path 434 due S over rough ground, climbing to Forcella Ambrizzola and rejoining the main route.

Screes below shapely Becco di Mezzodi (2603m) lead on to Forcella Col Duro (2293m), after which the path (436) crosses boulders and pasture down to Malga Prendera (2148m) under the great S cliffs of La Rochetta (2496m). Here keep R on path 458 and R again on path 467 at

1 hr - FORCELLA ROAN (2075m).

Wooded slopes and grassy terraces beneath Punta Puina bring us to Forcella della Puina (2034m) and a gentle descent over pasture to the track-end at Malga Durona and

30 mins - RIFUGIO CITTA DI FIUME (1917m) - *CAI Fiume section; 38 places; open beginning June to end-Sept; tel. 0437/720126.*

In the vicinity of the refuge there is a marvellous view between pine trees of Monte Pelmo's imposing N face - an immense wall of screes and rock rising 1000 metres to 3168m. Possible wild pitches in the area.

Leave the refuge S on path 472, dropping through forest to cross a rugged torrent bed, directly under Pelmo's glacier, high above. After a short descent, AV1 climbs over to

1 hr - FORCELLA STAULANZA (1773m) - *There is a privately owned bar-restaurant/refuge on this road pass.*

From the through-walker's point of view, the following section linking with the Monte Civetta massif leaves much to be desired. Neither of the two official alternatives manages to avoid several kilometres on rough roads, and the second routing described involves 250m of descent and subsequent ascent.

The first, and more straightforward, routing takes the road down SW from Forcella Staulanza for about 1km, turning off R at the first hairpin along a dusty, stony track, undulating through patchy forest. After about 2kms, fork L over the Rio Canedo stream, past Casera Vescova, under a ski-lift and climb round S between minor summits on Col di Baldi. The broad track continues SE past Roa Bianca's white outcrop and forks L down to the farm settlement of

1 hr - CASERE DI PIÒDA (1816m) - *milk, butter, cheese and bread for sale. Water just down the track. Good (if rough) car parking, including possible long-stay.*

The second routing is designed primarily for walkers wishing to explore Monte Pelmo by visiting Rifugio Venezia-De-Luca. (CAI *Venezia section; 60 places; open mid-June to mid-Sept; tel. 0436/9684.*) Monte Pelmo is one of the great peaks of the Dolomites, massive and commanding from all angles. Its huge southern recess, like some gargantuan armchair, is known as the *Caregón* and distinguishes it from afar. As long ago as 800BC, valley-dwelling huntsmen are believed to have reached the summit, though the first recorded ascent in recent times was made by that British pioneer John Ball in 1857. The normal route up is not particularly difficult but is a long and tiring climb.

At the path fork before Forcella Staulanza, AV1's alternative routing stays on path 472 which circles the S flanks of Pelmo to Rifugio Venezia. At Col delle Crepe, those wishing simply to proceed ahead to the Civetta massif should follow Rio Bianco down through forest to the road and Rifugio Palafavera (adjacent campsite). An old military road leaves opposite up through patchy forest and undergrowth and although at first its dog-legs can be short-cut, it must eventually be walked up to Casere di Piòda where the two alternatives rejoin. Allow 2 hrs from Forc. Staulanza.

From this rural scene with its herds of cows and goats ringing their bells melodiously from surrounding pastures, AV1 climbs determinedly up a well graded mule-track (many short-cuts) on the rocky N shoulder of Monte Coldai, an outlier of the Civetta. This is a hugely popular route, bearing numerous walkers of all shapes, sizes and dispositions on summer days. After two disappointing 'false tops', the path emerges suddenly at

1 hr 15 min - REFUGIO SONINO AL COLDAI (2132m) - *CAI Venezia section; 65 places; open mid-June to mid-Sept; tel. 0437/789160.*

The refuge is a good base for experienced climbers wishing to make an ascent of the Civetta (3220m). It was first climbed by an Englishman called Tuckett in 1867, but for a long time afterwards the sheer N wall defied ascent. Two more English climbers - Raynor and Phillmore - overcame the technical difficulties and scaled this face in 1895, since when a plethora of routes have become established, earning the mountain immense popularity.

The *Tivan* path from the refuge runs under the Civetta's E cliffs and onto the *via normale* and the *Alleghesi via ferrata*. Although an ascent of the peak is highly rewarding, it should only be attempted by experienced climbers since there are long, exposed stretches leading to a serious high-mountain environment.

Continue W up a small valley of white stone to cross Forcella Coldai - a lip of land revealing the stunning turquoise waters of Lago Coldai, encircled by little stony beaches. (Good wild pitches). On the L, Monte Civetta's northern spurs of Torre Coldai and Torre di Alleghe send up rock buttresses and towers, while to the N stands the now distant Tofane, its cable-car top station just visible.

AV1 drops round the lake's shore and passes over Forcella Col Negro (2203m) before losing height and entering Val Civetta. In a succession of overhanging slabs, peaks and pinnacles, the W face of Monte Civetta towers 1200m overhead and extends for 7kms in length - a marvellous sight which has been likened to huge organ pipes, the

Rifugio Coldai
beneath Monte Civetta's northern rock walls   53

'wall of walls', unique in the Alps. A hanging ice-field, the 'Cristalo', is suspended below the highest top.

Over undulating mountain terrain, the trail (on path 560) reaches 1 hr 45 min - **FORCELLA DI COL REÀN** (2107m).

The path leaving R (N) leads in 20 mins to Rifugio Attilio Tissi (2250m) - *CIA Belluno section; 35 places; open end-June to end-Sept. tel. 0437/723377.* The refuge stands close to the summit of Cima di Col Rèan (2281m), opposite the Civetta and high above Lago di Alleghe. A goods lift from the valley village of Masarè enables supplies to be sent up.

Long-distance walkers above Rifugio Coldai
Monte Pelmo, centre left

Lago Coldai

AV1 proceeds on down Val Civetta amidst a profusion of wild flowers, ignores paths off R and passes Col del Camp (1847m), whereupon it descends round the head of Valle di Foram, dominated by the square-cut tower of Torre Venezia (2337m). A short drop through pine trees on the good mule-track brings us to the spacious

1 hr 40 min - **RIFUGIO VAZZOLER** (1714m) - *CAI Conegliano section; 80 places; open mid-June to end-Sept.; tel. 0437/62163.*

Leaving N on the jeep track through thick forest (access to Agordo down this), AV1 rounds the head of Valle di Cantoni, with the fantastic shapes of Torre Trieste (2458m) and Cima della Busazza (2894m) ahead. When the track begins its zig-zagging descent down Val Corpassa, take path 554 off the second hairpin, climbing in mixed woodland to Forcella di Col Palanzin (1746m). Watching carefully for waymarks, continue over scree and rocks to gain the steep little

1 hr 30 min - **FORCELLA COL DELL'ORSO** (1826m).

Rising across boulders and thin pasture, AV1 arrives at the diminutive Casera del Camp (1861m) and turns abruptly E to reach Forcella del Camp (1933m), a break in the spur thrown south from the Moiazza to Monte Framont. Dropping in a wide curve before the

Rifugio Bruto Carestiato

Moiazza's great S face, the trail (path 554) passes the start of the *Gianni Costantini via ferrata* which heads up N into the scree and deep 'V' of cliffs to Bivacco M.Ghedini (2601m). From here it traverses the Moiazza'a summit ridge E and returns S to Rifugio Carestiato. Our wooded and more modest line continues E for another 2kms along the head of Val Framont and a short detour L brings us also to

1 hr 15 min - **RIFUGIO B. CARESTIATO** (1839m) - *CAI Agordo section; 40 places; open end-June to end-Sept; tel. 0437/62949. From the refuge are fine views down towards Agordo and over surrounding peaks, particularly the Tamer/San Sebastiano group to the E.*

Cutting off the first few zig-zags, our route follows a wide track along and down through more forest, easily reaching the grassy and pastoral

30 min - **PASSO DURAN** (1601m) - *and Rifugio S. Sebastiano -privately owned inn/refuge; 35 places; open mid-June to mid-Oct; tel. 0437/62360.*

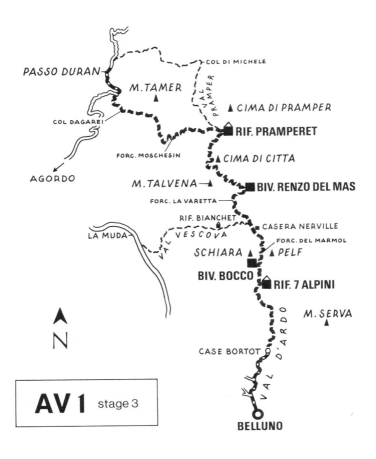

```
3000m ─────────────────────────────────────────────  3000m
               FORC. SUD DEL VAN DE CITTA
2500                                      SCHIARA        2500
        FORC. MOSCHESIN
2000                                                     2000
1500      RIF PRAMPERET            RIF. 7 ALPINI         1500
                       CAS. NERVILLE
1000  PASSO DURAN    BIV. RENZO              CASE BORTOT 1000
                     DEL MAS
 500                                                      500
                                              BELLUNO
  5 km
```

STAGE 3:
Passo Duran to Belluno

The wildest and loneliest stretch on Alta Via 1 begins with a climb through pine forest and a traverse along the rugged foot of the M. Tamer massif, an official variant passing round its other side on old hunting and forestry tracks. At Rifugio Pramperet, the route ascends to a rocky wilderness, an almost other-worldly landscape of bare, eroded limestone, before dropping briefly to softer regions at the head of a lovely wooded valley. The crossing of M. Schiara involves some technical difficulty and those wishing to avoid it can walk out down the valley to a road and buses for Belluno. For those walkers with climbing experience and a steady head, there is a thrilling descent down M. Schiara's south face on the 'Via Ferrata del Marmol'. From the refuge at its base, a cascading torrent is followed down, in and out of woods, to the roadhead above Belluno, thence on roads through outskirts to the town centre and journey's end.

★ ★ ★

NOTE: This final section traverses high, committing terrain, far from roads and with fewer than usual refuges. The traverse of Monte Schiara should only be undertaken by those with climbing experience and a good head for heights. Check the weather forecast before setting out (especially beyond Rifugio Pramperet) and be prepared to turn back or use a valley escape route if necessary. Ensure sufficient rations and protective clothing are carried and consider taking basic bivouac equipment.

58

(A variant skirts the N and E flanks of the Tamer/San Sebastiano group, to rejoin AV1 at Rifugio Pramperet. This *Zoldano Variant* is summarised after the main route reaches the refuge.)

From Passo Duran, AV1 descends S on the motor road for approx. 2kms to a bend at a torrent, which it crosses (car parking space). The path (543) leaves here, heading S, well waymarked and climbing through pine forest to

20 min -**FORC.DAGAREI** (1620m) - *There are distant views   between trees of the Pale di San Martino on AV2, from here seen side-on but actually a vast stony plateau.*

The little path meanders along between 1600m and 1700m, over boulder fields, meltwater ravines and scree, in and out of forest to

The distant Pale di San Martino on AV2
from Col Dagarei   59

Derelict wartime barracks,
Cima di Citta Ridge beyond

Malga Moschesin, some deserted barns just beyond the indistinct saddle pass near Col Pan d'Orso. (Possible shelter but no water). From here, a soundly constructed and well graded old mule-track, reminiscent of our packhorse roads, zig-zags up to a corner where an unexpectedly fine view is met of Monte Talvena (2542m) and Cima di Citta (2411m) across the deep cleft of Val Clusa.

Continue on round, past derelict barracks, ignoring a path L over bouldery grass, climbing a shallow stream bed up to

2½ hrs-3 hrs - **FORCELLA MOSCHESIN** (1940m) - *The views are magnificent: behind us, convoluted spires of limestone rise in tiers to Cima Moschesin, an outlier of Monte Tamer; to the N, Val Pramper and, if the weather is clear, the distant peak of Antelao (3263m).*

AV1 now follows the *Sentiero Balanzòle* which can be seen ahead dropping through thin forest and leading to a meadowy mule-track crossroads at Pra della Vedova. A little further E lies

1 hr - **RIFUGIO PRAMPERET** (1875m) - *Privately owned; 20-25 places; open 4/7 to 20/9; tel. 0437/78214. The refuge is a blend of the old and new extensions, its situation quiet and lonely. Wild camping allowed.*

Zoldano Variant from Passo Duran: this route, often following old hunting and forestry trails, has been waymarked recently by the Zoldana section of the CAI. It stays largely at 1500-1600m, circling the Tamer/San Sebastian group to reach Rifugio Pramperet up the densely wooded Val Pramper.

From Passo Duran, follow the road N for a short stretch and take a mule-track NE, over torrent beds, across the big screes of Pian Grand and through the wooded Col de le Buse (circa 1625m). Crossing the crest of Crode di Mezzodì and taking the higher path down over screes and patchy forest past Forcella de le Càure, the variant arrives at Casera Sopra il Sasso di San Sebastiano.

More forest leads up to Col di Michél (1491m) and a zig-zag descent to more open ground leading S into Val Pramper. The route threads along beneath the screes and vertical cliffs of Cima di Petorgnon, into more forest across Pian di Palui, where a mountain road is joined and followed for 1km to Pra della Vedova and thence to Rifugio Pramperet. Allow 6-7 hrs from Passo Duran.

From the path junction at Pra della Vedova, follow a good track (514) which climbs SW to the rocky Portela Piazedel (2097m). Grassy

Forcella Moschesin 61

Rock spires ('Campaniles')
Monte Tamer group

slopes are strewn with boulders as the route ascends to a rough open area, interspersed with snow patches and much scree from the towering Cima di Citta ridge above. Forcella Nord dei Van de Citta (2410m) is clearly visible ahead between Cima Nord and Cima di Mezzo, as views open out over the Agordino mountains and the nearer Castello di Moschesin.

Threading through rockfalls and zig-zagging up steep, rocky grass, a small pass is reached with marvellous views down Val dei Erbandoi to the W. Beyond a grassy shoulder and tiered rocks, the rough track levels off to arrive at the

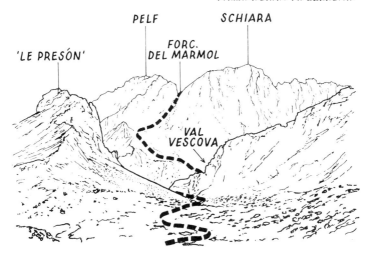

View ahead from the Van de Citta

2 hrs - **FORCELLA SUD DEL VAN DE CITTA** (2450m) - *on the connecting ridge between Cima di Citta (2465m) and Monte Talvena (2542m).*

Ahead stretches a primordial, almost lunar landscape of denuded rock, boulders and scree, the Van de Citta; in places it resembles Yorkshire limestone pavements but the scale is vast. Views are equally impressive - of Cima dei Bachet, Monte Talvena, the Pelf and the Schiara.

AV1 descends across this harsh environment where, incredibly, alpine flowers grow. Head towards a saddle between the rocky spine of 'Le Presón' to the L and Monte Talvena's bulk to the R, thereafter turning S down steep, broken rocks, and by a number of tortuous bends through crags and outcrops, drop steeply to pastureland at

1 hr - **PIAN DE FONTANA** (1632m) - *One of the barns here was converted to a permanent bivouac hut in 1976, the Bivacco Renzo del Mas, named after a Belluno climber who died on the Marmolada. There is no warden, but sleeping provision exists for 15 people, along with fireplace and running water.*

The trail continues its relentless descent (almost 1000m since the

63

Cima di Citta ridge), now over pasture to a path junction. (Path 520, L, provides a rapid escape route, following a torrent down Val dei Ross to a track and the main road in Val di Zoldo) AV1 trends W then S, climbing more steeply in zig-zags past a steep rock headwall to

1 hr - FORCELLA LA VARETTA (1704m) - *an idyllic spot in good weather, overlooking as it does the depths of Val dei Ross to the E and the hugely impressive N face of the Schiara to the S. The prominent notch of Forcella Marmol through which we pass is clearly visible. (A short distance W lies the deserted Casera la Varetta farmstead, useful shelter in emergency.)*

We now descend a small stony valley (good water source), re-emerge onto grassy slopes and contour round the head of Val Vescovà, maintaining height at around 1700m. After steep zig-zags we reach

40 min - SIGNED PATH JUNCTION.

Those walkers who have crossed Cima di Citta from Rifugio Pramperet should now take stock. The final push over the Schiara is far from a 'walk' in the normal sense of the word. Descending the S face involves some 600m (2000ft) of *via ferrata*, as the route cuts diagonally down the E end of the mountain. This well known *Via Ferrata del Marmol* is waymarked and equipped with iron ladders of various sizes, and lengths of anchored steel cable which, used in

Capercaillie

conjunction with a simple safeguarding technique (see introductory section) offer adequate protection. However, the descent is often very exposed, particularly in the lower sectors and the mountain walker with little or no climbing experience would need a more expert companion or guide and possibly the extra security of a rope. Bad weather or other factors might also militate against the crossing.

Having said that, the views and situations can be quite sensational and well worth the effort of the traverse. Indeed, other *via ferrata*, and rock routes to the Schiara's summit may be tackled, given the time and reasonable weather.

Variant avoiding the Schiara traverse: From the path junction, follow a well marked path (518), zig-zagging down W, over a torrent then mostly in woods to Pian dei Gat (1245m) - a forest clearing dominated still by the magnificent N prospect of the Schiara massif. Here stands the modern Rifugio Furio Bianchet *(Forestry Authority owned but run by CAI Belluno section; 46 places; open 10/6 to 30/9; tel. 0437/24077).*

The area is rich in geological interest, flora and fauna, all rigorously protected, and including chamois on surrounding crags and sometimes near the refuge itself.

Spotted Gentian

From here a forestry road (no private vehicles) leads down the attactive wooded valley to La Muda hamlet (483m) where there is an inn, telephone and bus service to Belluno. Allow about 3 hrs.

The final section of AV1 can be explored from Belluno by walking up Val d'Ardo as far as Rifugio 7 Alpini at the bottom of the Schiara rock wall.

From the path junction, the main route (path 514) proceeds SE (watch carefully for waymarks in vegetation at first), up out of trees to the modest

30 min - CASERA NERVILLE (1641m) - *possible shelter.*

Our route lies unequivocally before us, a steep ravine between the Schiara and to the L the Pelf (2506m). Flowery levels are left behind for slabs and rocky outcrops, scree and snow patches. 700m of stiff ascent, arduous but nowhere especially difficult, bring us to the

2 hrs - FORCELLA DEL MARMOL (2262m) - *a wild and airy place on the Schiara ridge.*

An apparently obvious way down is now confronted in the shape of the icy S gully, but it cannot be emphasised too strongly that this is both the incorrect line and a highly dangerous one. The CAI warn that there have been numerous accidents and several fatalities through people attempting a descent here.

Instead, look for paint flashes up the R wall towards the Schiara and quickly arrive at

15 min - BIVACCO DEL MARMOL 'SANDRO BOCCO' (2266m) *-CAI Dolo section; 9 places; permanently open. This small unsupervised metal shelter, installed in 1968 to the memory of a climber killed in a fall, offers a good starting point for climbs to the Schiara summit along the E ridge.*

There are wide views down into Val Belluna and of surrounding peaks as the descent route begins in earnest on the *Via Ferrata del Marmol* - a dizzy 600m of ledges and gullies, corners, buttresses and airy traverses. Well marked and aided, it leads down to an enormous overhanging cave called the *Porton* (1780m), whence easier grassy slopes drop to the conspicuous

3 hrs approx. - RIFUGIO 7th ALPINI (1490m) - *CAI Belluno section; 80 places; open mid-June to end-Sept; tel. 0437/20561. The refuge is set against an amphitheatre of rock walls bearing numerous climbing routes and vie ferrate. Indeed, this S wall is considered by some to form an ideal introduction to via ferrata climbing.*

The final descent to Belluno and civilisation lies down the scenic valley of the Ardo torrent, a clear watercourse of pools and cascades, crossed several times on bridges. The mule-track (501) clings in places to ledges cut into the ravine wall, at other times taking a line high above the torrent through delightful deciduous woods.

Just before the confluence of the Ardo and the Frét at Case Mariano (618m), we cross to the W side of the valley for the last time, joining path 506 to arrive at the tiny hamlet of

1½-2 hrs - **CASE BORTOT** (707m) - *This is the end of the motorable*

Near the roadhead in Val d'Ardo
Monte Serva top left

67

The Schiara (left)
and Pelf (right)
from Belluno's town centre

road from Belluno, with limited car parking space. There is also an inn and a telephone.

The remaining 1½-2 hrs of walking, first along hilly lanes then on suburban roads, might well prove more hazardous than the entire Alta Via just successfully negotiated! Compensations, however, include continuing wide views across Val d'Ardo to the distinctive cone of Monte Serva (2133m) rising above the first real farmsteads and settlements encountered since Passo Duran.

After walking out to the suburb of Bolzano Belluno, no-one will object if you catch a bus into

BELLUNO (400m) - *all supplies and services, including railway.*

The town is a fitting end to a classic Italian mountain route. Situated on the broad River Piave, it is a clean and charming place, chief town of the province and surrounded by high mountain massifs: to the N the Duranno, Schiara, Monte del Sole, the Pizzòc and the Vette Feltrine; to the S, a long pre-alpine chain culminates in Col Visentin (1763m), readily accessible via road, chair-lift to Col di Faverghera and an easy ridge walk SW. The view from this isolated southern vantage point is unique, ranging across the broad mass of the Dolomite range in the N to the Venetian Lagoon in the S. Col Visentin has been adopted as an optional extension to AV1.

Half a day could be profitably spent seeing Belluno's sights which include a number of buildings, piazzas and monuments of Renaissance and Venetian character. The Civic Museum contains fascinating Roman exhibits and there are several shady public gardens beckoning to the travel-weary!

Over the roofs of Belluno's fine town houses, the great south wall of the Schiara, now 10kms distant, still rises majestically, reminding us perhaps of the remarkable quality of the high level walk we have just completed.

★　★　★

ALTA VIA 2

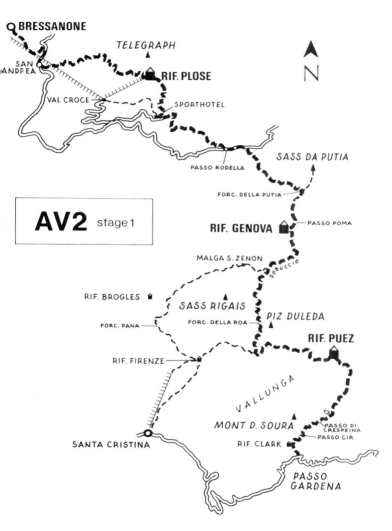

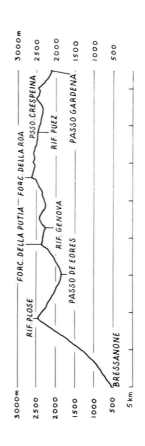

STAGE 1:
Bressanone to Passo Gardena

Nearly 2000 metres above historic Bressanone, on the southern fringe
of the Austrian Tyrol, Alta Via 2 begins its journey south at Rifugio
Plose, crossing meadows and forest before climbing a stony ravine to
the first col. Against a stunning backcloth of rock peaks and ridges in
the Puez Geisler Nature Park, and passing several refuges, the route
crosses a steep forcella and traverses rugged mountainsides onto a
limestone tableland. Rock pinnacles eroded into fantastic shapes lead
down to the winter skiing area of Passo Gardena.

*   *   *

From Bressanone's railway station forecourt with its little fountain,
the eye is drawn across Val d'Isarco, up beyond San Andrea's church
spire and intermediate levels of meadow and pine woods to the white
Rifugio Plose and the Telegraph summit, 2507m above sea level. Until
this barrier is surmounted, the limestone spires and crests of the Putia
and Odle massifs are obscured by a greener, more rounded
topography.

BRESSANONE (561m) - *all supplies and services; on road and rail
routes from the Brenner Pass. (NOTE: a campsite marked on some maps
no longer exists!)*

Bressanone is an elegant and charming town with a history dating
back more than a thousand years. It once belonged to the Roman
province of Rhoetia and has for centuries been a spiritual and cultural
centre. Its surroundings are characterised by ancient churches,
monasteries and notable buildings, with the old town itself still
medieval in appearance.

Shady, cobbled streets linked by narrow alleys and archways are
pervaded by a distinct flavour of Austria (we are at the southern edge
of the Tyrol), manifest in the rather up-market prices, the strudel and
cooked sausages, the leather breeches and feathered hats! Though
tariffs and currency are Italian, the Germanic tongue prevails.

Before leaving Bressanone, an important decision must be taken.
The official start of Alta Via 2 is from Rifugio Plose, reached from the
valley by a climb of some 1886 metres (6187 feet). This will take
between 5 and 6 hours, a testing introduction to any walk. Whilst for

Bressanone

the purist there may be no dilemma, the ascent being tackled with the necessary gusto, two alternatives for gaining this initial height do exist: one is a 21km drive on a good road to Val Croce (2040m, hotel, car parking), thence by a rough but motorable track or the footpath to Rifugio Plose. Another is to take the cable-car from Bressanone to Val Croce, continuing by path or chair-lift to the summit. Walkers should be forewarned, however, that neither cable-car nor chair-lift run regularly outside the skiing season.

The Isarco torrent, grey-green with meltwater, hurries through the town and is joined by the Rienza just to the S. For the ascent to the Plose on foot, leave the old town by an iron bridge across the Isarco (Ponte Aquila), turning R alongside the tumbling waters beneath trees in the Giardini Publici.

At the confluence of the Rienza and Isarco, cross another iron bridge L. (Turn R here, along Via Plose, for the cable-car station)

White Rockrose

Over the river, turn L along Lungo Rienza then R up Via Otto von Guggenberg at a sign for path No.4.

Pass a L fork, following a painted wall sign, and turn R again off a bend up a stony track (Via Trunt). At an electricity sub-station, fork R and in 150m fork R again, past a cross at a grassy area. Ignoring a L fork, the route proceeds along a level path past another crucifix, with views beginning to open out over Bressanone and surrounding peaks.

Continue along a lane by buildings, past cherry trees, turning off R at a bend by vegetable plots. The cable-car pylons are visible R, above the tree tops. Emerging onto a metalled lane, turn L at timber barns. Path 4 which we are following turns R, unmarked, up across a grassy bank, but Dorf hamlet is too pretty to short-cut. Look for a sign R, off a bend in the lane, proceeding along a track by more wooden barns and dwellings bright with geraniums. Go up by a grassy bank to join the road, turning R beneath the cable-car, over a torrent and into the village of

1 hr - **SAN ANDREA** (958m) - *provisions, bar/restaurants, post-office, car parking.*

San Andrea, ablaze with brightly coloured flowers in gardens and window boxes, is completely dominated by its imposing church, with frescoes and a very tall, slender spire.

Our route turns up L by a restaurant opposite a small car park threading between houses. At a junction we turn L and just beyond a cross-roads at the top of the village, a No.4 sign directs us over grass, across a stream and under the cable-car.

At an old wooden platform on the edge of forest, keep ahead through trees, ignoring a broad path L. Almost immediately fork half L off the main track, up a sunken path following waymarked trees. (Many other paths transect this area). Cross a stony forestry track and wind up in trees, past a spring by the path R, over another forestry track and on up in long zig-zags.

Turn R onto a path coming up from the L and pass a clearing (spring, possible wild camping). The route ascends through more broken forest and joins a jeep track, the gradient increasing. At a fork, bear R to a sign for the Plose below a new chalet and turn sharp L by a waymarked rock. Just beyond some timber sheds is a superb picnic spot near a stream, with a view SW down the Isarco valley through a gap in the tree cover.

Pass a path L signed 'Malga Buoi/Ochsenalpe 1 hr' and bear R.

After passing a ruined barn, cross the Brixen Hohenweg path and emerge at last onto open mountainside.

Rifugio Plose is clearly visible high on the ridge ahead and here two choices of route present themselves. Marginally easier is to turn up a path R, doubling back along the ridge. Path 4, however, proceeds straight ahead, indistinct on the ground but with occasional way-marked rocks. Zig-zagging up R of a rocky bluff, it becomes increasingly rough but nowhere difficult and eventually attains the ridge. Climb a wooden fence and walk under the chair-lift to a truly magnificent panorama over the bare rock summits of the Putia to the SE. A little way up to the L stands

4½-5 hrs - **RIGUGIO PLOSE** (2447m) - *CAI Alto Adige section; 50 places; open 1/6 to 31/10; tel. 0472/49333. (Possible long-term car parking.)*

Alta Via 2 officially begins here, as a sign on the refuge wall confirms. We set off L of the chair-lift station, along a track, L at a bend to keep to the cliff edge and down to a small forcella and a

10 min - **SIGNED PATH JUNCTION** (2383m).

*Sasso Putia (left) and the rock spires
of the Odle group, from Rifugio Plose*

77

Continue straight ahead (blue waymark), past a ski-lift building, winding down grassy hillside. Paths 4 and 6 are coincident here, but not very clear to follow. Watch for a rock waymarked *Skihütte No 6* and keep R of the ski-lift on a sketchy path towards a pond below. Go on down past dwarf junipers, firs and alpenrose and pass through a wooden fence. Descend to the bottom of a ski piste to a yellow sign, turning down L beneath a ski-lift, back under it again and down to a gate near the lift station. Here we join a road with several hotels, including the

1 hr 15 min - **SPORTHOTEL** (1894m).

(NOTE: This point may be reached from Val Croce on path 17 contouring E then SE, by-passing the Plose ridge and useful in bad weather. Approx 1 hr 30 min from Val Croce).

Turn L along the road which soon becomes the original muletrack, cross a stream and climb gently out above the tree line to a

25 min - **PATH JUNCTION** (2000m) - *at a crucifix and a sign for Enzianhütte*.

Follow the track down and at a further sign turn R on a delightful path descending through pine forest and over a stream (possible wild camping). The route continues on down towards the Halshütte, over several small streams, ignoring a path R to chalets, before finally reaching a metalled road at

30 min - **PASSO RODELLA** (1866m) - *The pass divides the Plose group from the Putia group but seems a minor feature.*

Turning L, a signboard announcing the 'Puez Geisler Nature Park' is passed and the road followed for about 10 min. At a bend and another sign, a path is taken R through level forest, over a bouldery torrent bed to a fork. The conspicuous narrow valley and forcella ahead, the Forcella della Putia, is our next goal.

Bear R at the fork, cross another torrent below a waterfall high to the R and climb steadily, joining with a path from the road below. At the foot of the steep little valley, our route crosses the torrent bed to its L bank (not as shown on some maps). The ascent is steady, on rock and loose scree, passing snow-choked gullies until, about 50m below the forcella, it crosses to the ravine's R bank. The shrill cry of marmots might be heard echoing from the enclosing cliffs. Soon, a grassy saddle and a crucifix appear ahead at

1½-2 hrs - **FORCELLA DELLA PUTIA** (2361m) - *a favourite spot*

The distant Tyrol from Forcella della Putia

for walkers and the starting point for an airy climb on Sass de Putia (2875m), directly above to the N. The steep ascent is very exposed towards the summit and is equipped with metal cable in places: views, however, are immense.

This pass, frequented by scavenging crows, provides a grand panorama. In the far SE rise the conspicuous peaks of the Tofane above Cortina on Alta Via 1; ahead to the S the entire N wall of the Puez massif, with a glimpse of the distant Sella group's snowfields peeping above.

Forcella della Putia and the distant Tyrol

Take path 4 (S), contouring hillside through small rocky outcrops, with the mountains of Alta Via 1 unfolding to the E. From a crucifix at Passo Poma (2344m), drop round R to arrive at

30 min - **RIFUGIO GENOVA** (2301m) - *CAI Alto Adige section; 60 places; open 1/7 to 30/9; tel. 0472/40132.*

Walk E from the refuge on path 3, back up to Passo Poma through drifts of wild flowers, proceeding S past a path R to Rifugio Gampen. AV2 takes a rising traverse across steep stony hillside to the crest of Sobuccio (2486m), where it turns R, slightly downhill. Ahead L stand the immensely impressive rock towers and snow-streaked screes of Punte del Puez. The conspicuous notch in the skyline to the S is Forcella della Roa, through which the route takes us.

Meanwhile, as we meander above the Alpe Medalges, contented cows chew the cud and chalets advertise milk and cheese for sale Before long, the path arrives at a small pass (Forcella San Zenon), with its almost obligatory crucifix, and a

Rifugio Genova   81

*Piz Duleda, top right (2909m) from the path
below Sobuccio*

40 min - **PATH JUNCTION** (2293m) - *From here, a variant drops W, skirting the precipitous needles of the Odle group to give marvellous views of its north faces. Rifugio Firenze is passed, with the nearby gondola-lift giving access to the town of Santa Cristina, before the variant rejoins the main route at Forcella Forces de Sielles (where details will be found).*

AV2 (path 3) continues S from the path junction, descending a little, before starting to mount over chalk-white rocky slopes beneath Forchetta Grande, crossing possible snow patches to round a rocky bluff (excellent view N).

The trail winds under the cliffs of Cresta di Longiaru and out across steep scree, whereafter extra care is needed. Beyond another rock outcrop lies a series of zig-zags on very steep scree leading to the forcella. Most of the late-lying snow in this gully is avoidable, but early in the season frozen snow here, as elsewhere on these high routes, may dictate carrying an ice-axe or staff. At the top we reach

1½-2 hrs - **FORCELLA DELLA ROA** (2616m).

Forcella della Roa

83

Through the pass, a path (*Sentiero della Piz Duleda*) leaves L, crossing a scree terrace near the foot of enclosing cliffs. This variant is for experienced climbers only, involving exposed scrambles and traverses, not all aided. It climbs to the ridge top of Piz Duleda (2909m), traversing S to join the main route W of the Alpe del Puez.

We leave Forcella della Roa, dropping S and ignoring a fork R down Val Roa (unless a visit is to be paid to Rifugio Firenza or Santa Cristina). After rough but mainly level ground, we start to rise, meeting path 2 up from Val Roa and swinging up zig-zags E to the well defined

1 hr - FORCELLA FORCES DE SIELLES (2512m).

Variant from Forcella San Zenon path junction: The path drops W in a series of loose zig-zags to thin forest and a herd of cows at Malga S. Zenon. Follow the rough road down for 200m, cutting bends to a stone bridge. Turn up L into forest (possible wild camping) on path 35, a popular route known as *Via delle Odle*. It meanders charmingly past wild flowers in abundance, including alpine clematis and alpenrose, all the time beneath the massive screes and rock peaks of the Odle group which show signs of major avalanche activity. Past a signpost and Nature Park board take the L fork. Ignore a path R by a chalet (possible shelter) and at a sandy knoll go down half-L and out over stony runnels.

A path junction is soon reached (water trough) - R to Santa Helena, L up to the difficult Forcella de Mesdi. Climbing ahead in broken forest, we reach a path L signed *Pana Scharte* (No.6), climbing on it past huge boulders and zig-zagging up scree, gradually trending W towards the narrow forcella, still hidden from view. The well graded path finally reaches the base of cliffs.

Rifugio Brogles can be seen below in its meadow but our route tackles the steep gully, to the R of a chimney at first, then up rock steps and stones, aided by metal pegs and ropes. There are chamois around the cliffs as we emerge at the top of

1 hr 30 min - FORCELLA PANA (PANA SCHARTE) - 2447m.

The contrast is astonishing, meadows stretching ahead to Val Gardena; beyond, the Sella group and the Marmolada. On path 1, aim at a small lake and in 10 min arrive at the Troier hut (meals, drinks, exceptionally fine crucifix).

Skirt R of the lake and at the top of a rise fork L to the

45 min - RIFUGIO FIRENZE (2039m) - *CAI; 90 places; open 1/6 to 15/10; tel. 0471/76307. A gondola-lift and track lead down to Santa Cristina, a smart, year-round resort (all supplies and services).*

Pass L in front of the refuge and drop to cross a stony ravine, climbing out and across a flat area. Ahead L can be seen the jagged, shapely summits of the Odle, rising to Sass Rigais. The path bends R, round the rocky corner of Montischella and into a vast, almost rectangular amphitheatre of scree and

Walkers on the Puez Plateau
Col Della Sonea distant top

cliffs. After climbing on path 2 for 500m, fork R up to the now obvious connection with the main route coming in from the N, which is met at Forcella Forces de Sielles. 1½ hrs from Rifugio Firenze .

The main route now turns sharp L (N), climbing beneath rocky outcrops then contouring on more steep scree. After traversing this exposed fan of shattered mountainside, climb over a lip onto easier ground, drop down the rock-strewn Alpe del Puez and wind along undulating terrain above cliffs on a natural platform high above Vallunga. The trail bends S round a spur of Col del Puez (2725m), trends E again over stream beds and round a stony corner to a grassy saddle and the buildings of

1 hr 30 min - **RIFUGIO PUEZ** (2475m) - *CAI Alto Adige section; 70 places; open 5/6 to 30/9; tel. 0471/85059. - access to Vallunga down path 1 (very steep, requires care). No doubt the refuge's isolated situation, far from jeep tracks, explains the inflated prices charged for food and drinks: it seems difficult to resent them in the circumstances!*

We have reached the heart of the extraordinary Puez group, a vast limestone upland wilderness scattered with snow patches, a desolate and primitive landscape whose ancient origins are revealed in its many fossil remains. Gradients are gentle, but because significant landmarks are few and far between, waymarking should be watched for carefully in poor visibility.

Path 2 (with 4) leaves SE from the refuge, rounding the head of Vallunga and veering S (R) at a junction with path 5/15. In about 1 km after a small descent, the path divides at Forcella di Campaccio (or Ciampai) - 2366m - path 4 dropping SE to the waters of Lago di Campaccio and down to Colfosco in the valley. Our route (path 2) climbs gently SW over the stony plateau, down to the vivid green waters of the tiny Lago di Crespeina, thereafter mounting steeply to the tall crucifix at

1 hr 45 min - **PASSO DI CRESPEINA** (2528m).

There is an exciting view ahead of the Sella massif, with its high square buttresses and snowfields, while down to the W, behind the monolithic Monte de Soura, lie the ski resorts of Val Gardena.

The path descends to an enclosed depression at the head of the small Val Chedul - keep to the L upper line, contouring easily along scree. (Possible wild camping, meltwater.) A short, sharp climb through rocks brings us up to Passo del Cir (2466m).

After zig-zags down the S side, the trail passes a remarkable forest of limestone spires (*campanile*), eroded into jagged, pocked pinnacles. We finally weave W down beneath the Pizzes da Cir cliffs into sloping meadows, past the smart timber Rifugio Clark and down a gravel track past hotels to the road at

1 hr - **PASSO GARDENA** (2137m) - *hotels, bar/restaurant, souvenirs, buses for Corvara, Bolzano, Cortina, Bressanone, Val Gardena, the Marmolada area, Passo Pordoi: mostly twice daily. Wild camping is possible but there is no natural water source and the area is very busy indeed in high season.*

Monte de Soura (left) and the Puez group from Passo di Crespeina

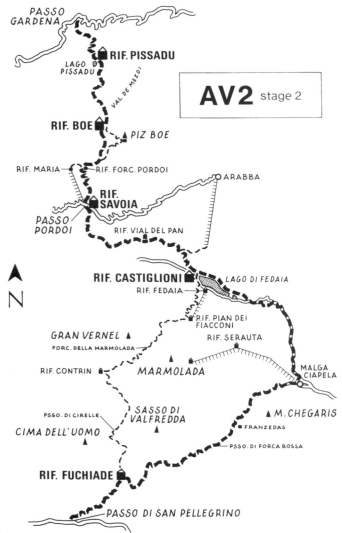

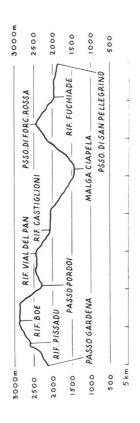

STAGE 2:
Passo Gardena to Passo di San Pellegrino

A sensational gully ascent leads into the Sella group, a wild and barren rock upland fringed by vertical cliffs and gorges. Two refuges are passed and a climb can be made to Piz Boè (3152m). An ancient grain-smuggling path is followed past several refuges, with exciting views of the glaciated Marmolada massif, highest mountain in the Dolomites range. Experienced and equipped climbers can traverse the Forcella della Marmolada beneath the soaring west ridge, while walkers circle to the east, with the option of a 3-stage cable car ride to Punta Rocca on the Marmolada summit. Climbers' and walkers' routes converge at Fuchiade, a popular summer beauty spot just above Passo di San Pellegrino.

★ ★ ★

From Passo Gardena, cross the road and take path 666 for the Pissadù and Boè refuges, contouring SE along stony slopes beneath the perpendicular walls of the Sella group. Unlikely though it seems at first, a manageable route does penetrate the massif - Val Setus. This narrow cleft gradually unfolds ahead R, its position betrayed by a stony scar of a path ascending from the large car park at a road hairpin below.

This is *via ferrata* country and is heavily patronised by enthusiasts of all shapes and sizes and levels of ability. One of the most popular of all *vie ferrata* - the *Tridentina* - starts a little further E at a waterfall.

Alta Via 2 turns into Val Setus, zig-zagging uncompromisingly up scree and over old snowdrifts. The trail is well marked and there are airy views down to the map-like road snaking up to Passo Gardena. Early in the season, when this north-facing gully is still snow-filled, the climb would be on snow and ice, requiring the appropriate skills and hardware.

Up ahead, the ravine narrows, curving to the L and steepening to a rocky scramble, aided but with no real difficulty.

NOTE: Try to avoid ascending Val Setus late on a fine weekend afternoon, as it is likely to be filled with crocodiles of people descending the rock section. Lower down, the more skilful and high-spirited will be scree-running or doing standing glissades on stretches

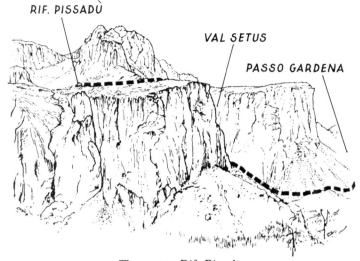

RIF. PISSADÙ

VAL SETUS

PASSO GARDENA

The route to Rif. Pissadù

of snow - all with varying degrees of competence and safety! Even the *Tridentina via ferrata* is crowded on public holidays, making an ascent long and potentially hazardous.

Once clear of the rock section, the route bears L (SE) to a forcella and over a broad shelf beneath Sass da Lec to

2 hr 15 min - RIFUGIO PISSADÙ (2583m) - *CAI Bologna section; 35 places; open beginning-June to end-Sept; tel. 0471/83292.*

Go down round the L shore of little Lago di Pissadù and proceed S across a long stretch of rugged mountainside, over rock (aided), scree and snow patches. We are climbing on path 666 along the W slopes of Cima Pissadù (2985m).

There follows a somewhat steeper ascent over more snow and scree, round W and up onto Altopiano del Meisules. At a broad col, path 666 joins 649 coming up across the rocky upland from Passo di Sella via Piz Selva. In a now S direction, cross l'Antersass and descend rough stony ground guided by cairns and poles to

3-3½ hrs - RIFUGIO BOÈ (2873m) - *CAI Trento section; 60 places; open beginning-July to mid-Sept; tel. 0471/83217.*

91

Rifugio Boè

Piz Boè

A few rocky steps, more snow, and the trail veers R, joining the descent from Piz Boè and contouring to the little Forcella Pordoi refuge at the top of a scree gully down which AV2 descends. *(Can be awkwardly blocked with snow at the top - care needed.)* Steep scree soon eases, broadening out as the clear path drops down the mountainside, crosses a grassy hill and arrives at

1 hr 45 min - **PASSO PORDOI** (2242m) - *bars, restaurants, hotels, telephone, souvenirs galore, buses (for Arabba, Canazei, Passo di Sella) Albergo/Refugio Savoia; 45 places: open beginning June to mid-Oct; tel. 0462/61279. A German military mausoleum commemorating the dead of World War I lies 2 kms along a minor road to the E.*

NOTE: An easier descent from Forcella Pordoi (depending on weather, energy levels and conscience) is to climb W (waymarked) to Rifugio Maria on Sass Pordoi (2952m). Here too, meals, drinks and accommodation may be obtained and Passo Pordoi reached effortlessly by cable-car.

Leaving Passo Pordoi, we enter the Marmolada group and its volcanic spur, first taking path 601, the celebrated *Vial del Pan*. In the 17th century the Venetian republic became extremely jealous of its grain trade from southern Italy and prohibited the local population from selling maize flour. This route was used to smuggle grain through the Bellunese and Romansch valleys.

The path begins between the Rifugio Savoia and an associated bar/restaurant, forking R before a small chapel and climbing easy slopes beneath Sass Beccé (2538m). It is a popular walk and well signed, leading past a couple of small, privately-owned huts to undulate along the S flank of Col del Cuc, with magnificent views across the deep Avisio valley to the glaciated Marmolada and adjacent Gran Vernel.

These great peaks are the loftiest summits in the whole Dolomites region, a prodigious mountain barrier which south-bound walkers need to cross or circumvent. To the N, before sight of them is lost, are good views back to Passo Pordoi and Piz Boè. Contouring grassy hillsides, the track reaches

1 hr - **RIFUGIO VIAL DEL PAN** (2432m) - *privately owned; meals, drinks.*

After about 2kms of mainly level path, a junction is reached. The L fork continues above a line of rocky bluffs below the steep cliffs of Belvedere (2650m) and round NE to the hut and top station of a cable-

On the trail above Val Lasties

Walkers at Rifugio Vial del Pan enjoying a spectacular view of the Marmolada

car from Arabba *(provisions, Post Office, cafes, bars, chemist, buses).*
Alta Via 2 takes the R fork, dropping in zig-zags round the rocky
bluffs to the W end of the lovely Lago di Fedaia. It is an artificial lake
and by the dam stands the

50 min - **RIFUGIO CASTIGLIONI** (2054m) - *CAI Sede Centrale
section; 85 places; open all year; tel. 0462/61117. Accommodation here is
in great demand - reservation essential!*

The main walking route describes a wide arc to the E of the
Marmolada, but an option for those with the necessary experience and
given suitable weather conditions, crosses the Forcella della
Marmolada. This is not an ordinary walking itinerary and requires at
least some mountaineering skill and equipment: ice-axe, crampons
and rope, glacier cream and goggles. This route is described first, as
far as Rifugio Fuchiade near which the two alternatives rejoin, but the
Marmolada is such a significant landmark to have reached that a little
extra information would not go amiss.

The huge limestone massif, 1000 metres high along some of the

5kms of its south face, is capped by the largest glacier in the Eastern Alps. Its moraines carry the imprints of many fossils while on the mountain itself there is a predominance of high, grey rock slabs and smooth vertical gullies.

The Marmolada was first attempted (unsuccessfully) in 1830 by Italian climbers from the Livinallongo valley and in 1860 by the English climber John Ball, who managed to reach Punta Rocca (3309m), lower of the two summits. 4 years later, Paul Grohmann from Austria, accompanied by Italian guides, reached Punta Penia itself (3340m).

During the spring of 1916 and again in the summer of 1917, the Marmolada witnessed fierce hand-to-hand fighting between Austrian and Italian troops. It was a perpetual contest for positional superiority, with action by small patrols over very difficult terrain, often in appalling weather conditions.

To escape enemy fire, the Austrians excavated an ingenious complex of galleries some 8kms in total length, within the glacier itself: it proved spacious enough to shelter a whole battalion. To

Lago di Fedaia
Monte Civetta (on AVI) distant right

individual acts of daring and heroism on both sides was added the constant threat from storm and avalanche which claimed many hundreds of lives, particularly in 1916. It is still possible today to find cave openings, the remnants of paths, commando posts and barracks on the mountainsides.

CLIMBERS' ROUTE: Cross the dam from Rifugio Castiglioni to the valley station of the glacier chair-lift. Either take this, or climb up past the ruined Rifugio Col dei Bous and thence over rock and scree to reach

2½ hrs *(on foot)* - **RIFUGIO PIAN DEI FIACCONI** - *privately owned; 25 places; open mid-Feb. to end-Sept; tel. 0462/61412.*

From Pian dei Fiacconi it is necessary to descend first, losing considerable height, before the thin track veers W. The glacier has retreated since maps were surveyed and the route now crosses glaciated rock, snow and ice patches at easy gradients in a corrie to where the NW crest of the Marmolada drops as a great sharp-edged ridge of rock. Skirt S round beneath this, then mount the steep glacier and shattered rocks (route depending on conditions) up to

2½-3½ hrs -**FORCELLA DELLA MARMOLADA** (2910m) -*a narrow notch*

Near the Marmolada summit with
Sasso Lungo distant right

Punta Rocca (left) Marmolada's lower summit   Sasso Lungo distant right

between Piccolo Vernel and the W ridge of Punta Penia (climbable from here on the 'Via Ferrata Marmolada').

There follows an aided 20m vertical rock descent down a narrow gully, then a big drop down extensive scree zig-zags. Pass a junction with path 610, keep R (W) over more scree and thin pasture down to

1½ hr - **RIFUGIO CONTRIN** (2016m) - *privately owned; 80 places; open mid-June to mid-Sept; tel. 0462/61101.*

From Malga Contrin, a little E of the refuge, take path 607 at a junction, meandering S over torrent beds. After a short and steeper section, another path junction is reached at which we turn sharp L (SE) up a rising spur. In about 2kms we arrive at a small col (2440m) where a trail leaves L for Pàsso Ombrettola. Continue on path 607 (SW) up a broad valley of fallen rock debris towards a gap in the skyline ahead -

2 hrs approx. - **PASSO DI CIRELLE** (2683m).

AV2 descends steep scree *(possible snow patches require care)* and after a narrow passage by a large rock to the R, zig-zags down stony slopes to a bouldery depression. It is important here to avoid going farther R still, down more scree: instead, take the winding path down flowery hillsides to a stream.

There are fenced-off areas and notices warning of unexploded bombs; the author once witnessed lines of troops carrying out a clearance exercise and the occasional loud 'boom' accompanied the walk for many kilometres ahead!

Steep screes below
Passo delle Cirelle

Presumably the area is much safer now and backpackers should not be deterred from pitching near the stream! A good path through lush meadows leads to

1 hr - **RIFUGIO FUCHIADE** (1972m) - *privately owned; 8 places; open mid-June to mid-Sept; tel. 0462/64014.*

WALKERS' ROUTE: From Rifugio Castiglioni, follow the track along Lago di Fedaia's N shore, past a smaller lake beyond the dam, to reach the road at an inn/refuge.

At and below Passo Fedaia are the scars of road works which, whilst improving the dangerously narrow and dilapidated old road at Pian de Lobbia, will inevitably disturb the line of AV2 which was routed along it. It may be possible to descend from the pass on a ski piste beneath angled rock slabs under Sass del Mulo and thence down to the Capanna Bill hut. When completed, the new road might leave the old one as a pedestrian way in places. In any case, it is best further down to walk on ski piste and grass verges rather than the road itself, passing several bars and huts to arrive at

Spring Gentian

1 hr 30 min - **MALGA CIAPELA** (1446m) - *hotels, bars, restaurants, car parking, campsite, limited provisions.*

Malga Ciapela, a smart though small tourist development, would make an excellent base for exploring the Marmolada and peaks to the W and S, criss-crossed by numerous paths.

The 3-stage cable-car ascent to Rifugio Punta Rocca (3259m) near the Marmolada summit is highly recommended; although not cheap, it represents good value, for the ride up is sensational. Above Rifugio Serauta (2876m), the half-way station, the edge of the Marmolada glacier is crossed and from the top station (meals, drinks, etc.) a snowy ridge leads west for some 200m, with exceptionally far-reaching views in all directions, given good visibility. Temperature, wind speed and visibility are noted on a blackboard, along with cable-car running times, at the valley station.

AV2 passes the cable-car entrance at Malga Ciapela, drops a little to a lane R alongside the Pettorina torrent and passes a campsite. A popular cross-country ski route in winter, the metalled lane soon becomes a forest track. Beyond wooden farm buildings, cross a torrent at car parking space, ignore a path off L and continue ahead up the broad, rough track.

Pass a signed path R (610) for Rifugios Falier and Contrin and when a signed junction is reached, keep up R. At the next bend, turn L (signed Forcella Rossa) - there is a fine view of the Marmolada's vast south wall leading E to Piz Serauta (3035m).

More relentless zig-zags take us up through thinning forest (increasingly open views E to Monte Chegaris) until, just short of barns at Franzedas and before a 90 degree bend in the track crosses a stream, turn up R (waymarked with stones and wood, thereafter red and white paint flashes).

The crude new jeep track we have followed has obliterated much of the original mule-track until now, but from here this ancient and well constructed way leads us up across a bouldery alp, over the infant Pettorina, through more conifers and across earthy slopes, finally zig-zagging SW up to the broad

2½-3 hrs - **PASSO DI FORCA ROSSA** (2490m).

Still heading SW, AV2 descends past reddish slopes, through undulating and rough stony pastures before slanting up a grassy ridge which it crosses lower down. Swinging round past several path intersections, we join meadows and a motorable track at Rifugio

Fuchiade, after which climbers' and walkers' routes are coincident.

The Cigole valley head lies beneath a wall of peaks, from (W to E) Cima del Uomo (3010m) to Sasso di Valfredda (3002m). It contains many timber chalets and is a popular picnic destination with Italian families who can drive up the grit track from Passo di San Pellegrino. Grassy meadows are ablaze with colourful wild flowers which seem to survive despite the Italian appetite for picking them to take home!

From the refuge, fork R and follow the track down (some car parking spaces), past the Albergo Mirago adjacent to the diminutive Lago di Pozze, to arrive at

1 hr 45 min - **PASSO DI SAN PELLEGRINO** (1919m) - *bar/restaurant, car parking, telephone, bus service.*

Sasso di Valfredda (top left-centre)
from Fuchiade

105

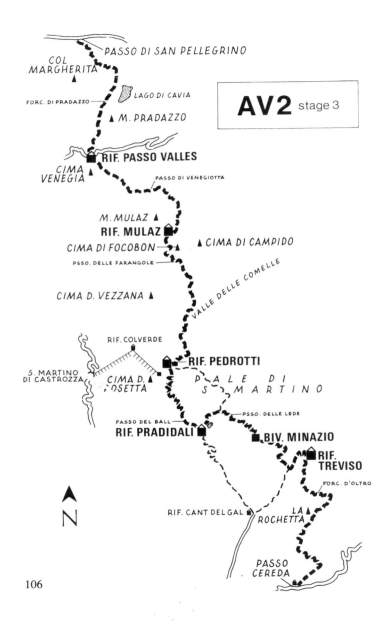

PASSO DI SAN PELLEGRINO

COL MARGHERITA ▲

FORC. DI PRADAZZO

LAGO DI CAVIA

AV2 stage 3

▲ M. PRADAZZO

RIF. PASSO VALLES

CIMA VENEGIA ▲

PASSO DI VENEGIOTTA

M. MULAZ ▲

RIF. MULAZ

CIMA DI FOCOBON ▲

▲ CIMA DI CAMPIDO

PSSO. DELLE FARANGOLE

CIMA D. VEZZANA ▲

VALLE DELLE COMELLE

RIF. COLVERDE

RIF. PEDROTTI

S. MARTINO DI CASTROZZA

CIMA D. ROSETTA

P A L E   D I   S   M A R T I N O

PASSO DEL BALL

PSSO. DELLE LEDE

RIF. PRADIDALI

BIV. MINAZIO

RIF. TREVISO

FORC. D'OLTRO

RIF. CANT DEL GAL

LA ROCHETTA

PASSO CEREDA

▲ N

106

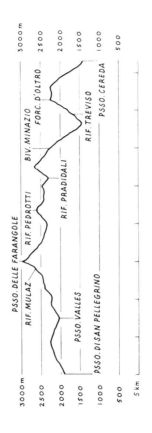

107

STAGE 3:
Passo di San Pellegrino to Passo Cereda

Crossing boulder-strewn upland above a delightful lake, AV2 drops to a road pass before commencing a particularly rugged section over the highest point on either Alta Via - a pass at 2932 metres. The walker is led through a landscape of incredible rock peaks and past a high refuge as the path, aided on several stretches, climbs to the Pale di San Martino plateau. This vast and ancient limestone tableland, once a coral lagoon, is transected by many paths radiating from a popular refuge and forms part of a Nature Reserve above the smart ski resort of San Martino di Castrozza. A stony descent is followed by rock ledges to a pass and arrival at another refuge, set by a mountain lake and surrounded by rock spires. Beyond the next rugged pass, AV2 loses 1000 metres of altitude, passing a bivouac hut and reaching the last refuge on this stage, situated in dense forest. A steep, high forcella and a traverse beneath crags and rock faces brings us down to meadows and thence to the road and farmland at Passo Cereda.

* * *

Passo di San Pellegrino is being developed for skiers and tourists and is paying the inevitable price in desecration. A new cable-car runs to the porphyry rock mass of Col Margherita (2550m), a singularly unattractive summit for these parts, and a new ski piste has been bulldozed up to the col used by AV2 near Cima Pale di Gargol.

Leave the pass across a big car park on path 658, signed Passo Valles. Bear L and proceed up through thin bushy forest, eventually climbing more steeply through rock outcrops to arrive at the col.

Ahead lies a grassy upland strewn with large granite boulders - the Altipiano degli Zingari - and below us Lago di Cavia. In normal visibility there are no route-finding problems, but in mist watch carefully for waymarks. Following above the lake's W bank, there is an easy climb to Forcella di Pradazzo (2220m), with magnificent views ahead to the Pale di San Martino. The path joins a motorable track winding down past Malga Pradazzo to

2½-3 hrs - **PASSO DI VALLES** (2031m) - *and Rifugio Passo Valles, 30 places; open all year; tel. 0437/50270. Also bar/restaurant, telephone, car parking and resident St.Bernard dog!*

On the trail above Passo di Valles

Chapel at Passo di Valles

AV2 climbs SE from the pass, at first badly eroded then angling L up the slopes of Cima Valles O Venegia (2305m). Ahead are the big red-sandstone striated cliffs of Cima del Lago (2313m).

(At the first little pass (Forcella di Venegia), a path fork R (749) links with a rough road in Val di Venegiotta, offering a possible bad weather route to San Martino di Castrozza via path 712 and the main road (short-cut by paths). The main route can then be rejoined by taking the chair-lift and cable-car to the plateau a short distance from Rifugio Pedrotti. This unofficial alternative also by-passes the steep and in places exposed *Sentiero delle Farangole*, the highest point reached on either Alta Via.)

On these grassy, almost British hillsides can be found the Arctic Poppy and the Large-flowered Leopardsbane, as well as occasional heather and ling. The route bears L along and behind the crest of Cima del Lago and passes a tiny lake where, with luck, the walker will spot or hear marmots which inhabit this area.

There are superb views ahead of Monte Mulaz (2906m) and Cima di Val Grande (2985m) with its little hanging glacier fringed with green ice.

AV2 descends shattered mountainside and turns a rocky corner up to

1 hr - **PASSO DI VENEGIOTTA** (2303m) - *There is access R on path 751 (which divides here) down to a N branch of Val di Venegiotta, hemmed in to the E by a breathtaking rampart of snow-streaked rock towers and walls.*

Going E on path 751, we climb up and round a rocky spur, crossing the steep N slopes of the Monte Mulaz ridge to the small Passo del Fochetti di Focoben. (Junction with path 753 going E to Val Focobon.) There are magnificent panoramas N and E over Val Focobon, and the incredible *campaniles* (rock spires) of Cima del Focobon are progressively revealed to the S.

Descend R across a steep slope and on down with care over broken rock in a circular depression above the cliffs and screes at the head of Val Focobon. The route zig-zags up to a small bowl-shaped valley, often snow-filled. Depending upon the quantity and disposition of the snow, the path takes a line L across it, onto moraine and up to a small grassy alp. Following waymarks, we traverse steep little gullies and terraces, no more than easy scrambles, finally ascending broad, ice-smoothed slabs to the small Forcella Arduini.

*View from Forc. di Venegia
towards Cima di Val Grande*

111

Rifugio Mulaz

With the Focobon glacier and the fantastic rock profiles of Cima di Focobon (3056m) and Cima di Campido (3001m) now close at hand, another short climb followed by almost level terrain brings us to

3-4 hrs - RIFUGIO MULAZ (2571m) - *CAI, S.Marco Frezzeria section; 65 places; open beginning July to mid-Sept; tel. 0437/50184.*

From the refuge's rocky platform, well marked and straight-forward tracks climb to the summits of Monte Mulaz (2819m) in 45 mins and Sasso Arduini (2582m) in 10 mins.

Amongst tracks radiating from here, AV2 looks rather unlikely a line. Indeed the following stretch - some 7kms (4 hrs) known as *Sentiero delle Farangole* - to attain the Pale di San Martino plateau requires a steady head and secure movement. It traverses steep and

112

loose ground in many places but is well waymarked and most of the more exposed sections are provided with metal cables and handrails.

From the refuge, climb towards Passo del Mulaz (2619m), forking L at a sign and scrambling up extremely steep scree to a small gap in the NW crest of Cima di Focobon called Forcella la Margherita. Now on the other side of the ridge, the path climbs W, then round E towards the Campanile di Focobon, a forest of amazing rock shapes.

A clear-cut notch in the jagged crest above is reached by climbing broken rock, boulders and snow patches (aided), with loose stones making the going decidedly tricky in places! This is the highest point reached on the whole of AV1 and AV2 -

1-1½ hrs - **PASSO DELLE FARANGOLE** (2932m.)

Through the pass, the ground drops away to unseen depths in Valle delle Comelle, which cuts a deep trench SW into the plateau. Descend a short rock pitch (aided) at the northern extremity of the small Ziroccole glacier and bear R over rock-strewn slopes and scree enclosed between soaring precipices. Proceeding S along rugged

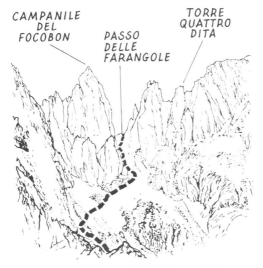

Part of 'Sentiero Delle Farangole'
the highest stretch on AV2

Rifugio Pedrotti (right) Rifugio Rosetta (centre)
Cima della Rosetta (top left)

mountainside, the waymarked path drops down the R side of Val Grande, round the base of the Torcia di Val Grande campanile, and into the circular hollow of Val Strutt.

The trail, exposed in places and equipped with metal cable where necessary, contours along to the head of Valle delle Comelle above crags on a stony, grassy shelf. Dropping to Pian dei Cantoni, we join path 704 rising from the valley, climbing SE up the rocky valley head with no more technical difficulties. We soon emerge onto the vast limestone tableland of the Altepiano delle Pale di San Martino, mounting successive rocky steps up to

2½-3 hrs - **RIFUGIO GIOVANNI PEDROTTI** - *CAI Trento section; 108 places; open mid-May to end-Sept; tel. 0439/68308.*

1km SW stands the top station of the Rosetta cable-car (bar, meals, accommodation in Rifugio Rosetta). If you are hankering after haute-couture clothes, expensive perfume and watches, the ride down to chic San Martino di Castrozza is a must! Luckily for the walker on AV2, there are also banks, hotels, bars, restaurants, Post Office, chemist, food shops, a campsite and buses. The cable-car takes you to

Looking back down Valle delle Comelle from the Pale di San Martino plateau

Colverde, whence there is a sensational chair-lift to the valley.

Beyond the Rosetta top station lies a slanting plane of rock leading easily to the summit crucifix of Cima della Rosetta (2243m). If circumstances allow, an ascent (approx. 30 mins) is strongly urged, for views over the extraordinary Pale di San Martino are vast and high mountains can be seen in all directions. There are also vertiginous views down to San Martino over 1200m below, the western edge of the plateau being sheer and precipitous.

The Pale di San Martino is a dissected, rolling upland of grey limestone, edged with rock peaks - its geological origin the inner lagoon of a coral atoll. Even the Puez tableland already encountered is dwarfed by the scale here.

Early in the season, when the surface is still piebald with snow patches, there is no vestige of greenery as far as the eye can see, except in glimpses of distant valleys. Yet, close to, this unlikely habitat supports a host of miniature alpine flora. The tiny blooms flourish in crevices and little protected corners away from paths which radiate from Rifugio Pedrotti.

On the summit of Cima della Rosetta ▸

116
Croda della Pala (top left)
on the western edge of the Pale di San Martino

Golden Eagle

Paths themselves, for all their signposting and waymarks, are only scratchings across this hard crust of land - they are discernable where the stone is a little broken and browned from the passage of boots and where snow is bisected by a dirty groove of steps, until it disappears under the summer sunshine.

From Rifugio Pedrotti, AV2 (now path 702) is well signed S, first over undulating limestone following a water supply pipe as far Passo di Val di Roda, then down many steep, stony zig-zags built into the loose slopes - almost 300m of descent.

The broad path rounds crags beneath Cima di Val di Roda on a ledge, crossing a gully on a little wooden footbridge before traversing

Passo del Ball (top right)
and its approaches

*Enjoying a minestrone
at Rifugio Pradidali*

scree and possible snow patches. A path R (702) drops to the valley.
We now follow a ledge cut into the rock face (aided for about 100m),
with Passo del Ball a conspicuous notch ahead. The final slopes are
likely to be across snow, but quantities vary from year to year.

From Passo del Ball (2443m) the gradient is easier, down beneath
the cliffs of Torre Pradidali (2553m) and round over a rocky bluff to

2-2½ hrs - **RIFUGIO PRADIDALI** (2278m) - *CAI Treviso section; 70
places; open mid- June to end Sept; tel. 0439/67290. The refuge's interior
is full of character, a dark womb of varnished timber with a glazed balcony
overlooking a roughly circular basin bounded by screes, gullies and soaring
rock towers. These summits are eroded into fantastic sharpened forms - the
Campanile di Pradidali - and the whole mountain mass S from here is
threaded by many vie ferrate.*

(From the refuge, an interesting variant leads to Rifugio Treviso by
dropping into Val Canali (bar/restaurants/campsite), thus circum-
venting continuing high ground and offering a pleasant contrast of
itinerary, especially in poor weather. Details appear when the main
route reaches Rifugio Treviso.)

AV2 now leads off N past sombre Lago Pradidali and climbs to a
signed junction where we fork R on path 711. (Path 709 comes in from
120

the NE and offers a possible short-cut to here, having climbed across the plateau from Rifugio Pedrotti over snowfields and rock. In mist, however, it is not advised.)

Our route, now E, scrambles up a rocky ledge to the edge of a stony terrace, then up steeper broken rock before the gradient levels off as we approach the narrow

1-1½ hrs **PASSO DELLE LEDE** (2640m).

Our path now descends, relentlessly and steeply, first down a gully then SE across scree and rocks at the head of Vallon delle Lede. Winding on down its L side to grassy alps, we trend R and drop to a small bivouac hut, invisible until the last moment -

45 min - **BIVACCO CARLO MINAZIO** (2250m).

Keeping still to the ravine's L side, heading towards Pala dei Colombi's enclosing walls, AV2 crosses gullies down steeper rock and boulder slopes to a junction at the edge of thin forest. Here turn sharp R (SW) down through conifers, climbing round stream beds and veering SE before finally emerging at the rough road in Val Canali.

Turn L upstream on path 707 from Cant del Gal and where the track gives out, climb R up zig-zags in dense forest to

1-1½ hrs - **RIFUGIO TREVISO** (1631m) - *CAI Treviso section; 35 places; open beginning June to end Sept; tel; 0439/62311.*

VARIANT FROM RIFUGIO PRADIDALI: Descend S on path 709, zig-zagging down the steep head of Val Pradidali, over possible snow-banks, reaching pine forest and easier gradients. A good track (still 709) is followed down, crossing the torrent and leading to inns and restaurants at Cant del Gal. (Road head with car parking space, bus service to Fiera di Primiero, campsite 3kms S.)

Turn sharp L up Val Canali on the forestry road to join the main route in about 3kms, thence climbing to Rifugio Treviso.

NOTE: For those wishing to avoid the following steep traverse of Forcella d'Oltro, descend Val Canali towards the main road, taking path 738 on the L (E) near a shrine at a stream and climb round the ridge's S end to reach the main road just W of Passo Cereda. Buses could be used.

AV2 continues S from Rifugio Treviso, undulating through dwarf conifers and crossing several deep torrent beds. The path trends SE, leaving the upper limit of trees and climbing over rocks and scree, increasingly more E up towards the well defined forcella in the ridge

121

wall ahead. The approaches are steep, among boulders and on stony grass, leading to

1½-2 hrs - **FORCELLA D'OLTRO** (2120m) - *almost a double pass, divided by an unusual point of rock. The ridge we are crossing is quite narrow so that views from the forcella extend W and E over valleys far below.*

Still on tricky terrain requiring care, follow waymarking E for approximately 200m, forking sharp R (SW) and soon beginning to ascend again, along beneath the crags and rock faces of Cima d'Oltro, La Rochetta and Cima Feltraio for about 2kms. Several steep gullies are encountered.

At a small valley head in a region of oddly shaped rocks, the path veers SE and climbs to a little gap, passing thence to the R of the smallest rock tower (Campanile de Regade). A descent over stony and grassy slopes leads down to the ruined Casera Regade (1683m), with views ahead opening out to Piz di Sagron (2486m) and Sass de Mura (2522m).

Negotiating the steep slope diagonally L, we reach woods, pass a steep gully choked with clay-smeared boulders and emerge at the flowery Bastie meadows and a good track. Turn R and in 1km arrive

122   *Near Lago Pradidali*

at the main road and

2-2½ hrs - **PASSO CEREDA** (1361m) - *and Rifugio Cereda, privately owned; 40 places; open all year; tel. 0439/62133. On the main road between Gosaldo and Fiera di Primiero. Buses.*

Unlike other major road passes so far encountered, Passo Cereda is agricultural in character, though winter snow cover brings a new lease of life to the area in the form of skiing.

Pasque flower

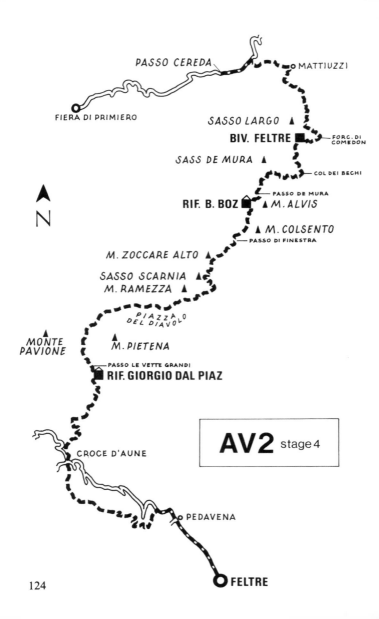

PASSO CEREDA

MATTIUZZI

FIERA DI PRIMIERO

SASSO LARGO ▲

BIV. FELTRE ■ FORC. DI COMEDON

SASS DE MURA ▲

COL DEI BECHI

PASSO DE MURA

RIF. B. BOZ ◆ ▲ M. ALVIS

▲ M. COLSENTO

PASSO DI FINESTRA

M. ZOCCARE ALTO ▲

SASSO SCARNIA ▲▲
M. RAMEZZA ▲

▲ N

PIAZZA
DEL DIAVOLO

MONTE
PAVIONE ▲

▲ M. PIETENA

PASSO LE VETTE GRANDI

RIF. GIORGIO DAL PIAZ

CROCE D'AUNE

AV2 stage 4

PEDAVENA

124

FELTRE

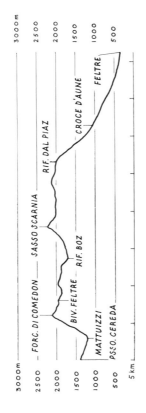

125

STAGE 4:
Passo Cereda to Feltre

The final stage traverses the Feltrini Alps, at the southern extremity of the Dolomites. It is solitary, wild country, largely waterless but surprisingly vegetated, especially on south-facing slopes. Leaving the village of Mattiuzzi, we climb past the scene of a major landslip to a well-appointed bivouac hut. The route threads along beneath mountain walls, passing large caves before arriving at the first of only two refuges in this stage. Following a ridge honeycombed with World War I tunnels, we climb to the summit of Sasso Scarnia and descend towards the Piazza del Diavolo, an extraordinary area of huge boulders which is also rich in wildlife: one of three nature reserves in the Feltrini Dolomites. A broad track and easier gradients lead to the final mountain pass and the second refuge, whereafter an old military road drops steadily to the heights above Pedavena suburb. It is then but a short distance to the old walled town of Feltre, with its Renaissance architecture and flavours of the Venetian plain which stretches south towards the Adriatic sea.

★   ★   ★

NOTE: This final stage of AV2 comprises a trek across the largely unfrequented and remote Feltrini Dolomites. Summits range between 2000m and 2300m, very rugged and steep on their north sides but sloping gently to the south into a vast upland dotted with great grassy hollows. Often these contain isolated monoliths or large rock slabs created by the action of ice over thousands of years.

Some believe that this stage is an afterthought, simply a device to bring the route to its conclusion at a sizeable town worthy of nomination as the southern terminus. However, the range forms an interesting contrast with those already walked through and thus avoids mere repetition. Even though it maintains height at around 2000m, the path transects mountainsides often covered with scrub and vegetation or meadows thick with wild flowers.

The crossing will take about 3 days and since there are only 2 refuges and 1 bivouac hut, walkers should pause and take stock. Safe descents from the massif may only be made in about three places, so if

Devil's Claw

the weather threatens (and it tends to be less stable here, close to damp winds rising from the Venetian Plain), escape from high ground can be problematic. If these or other reasons indicate that discretion may be the better part of valour, AV2 can be finished here at Passo Cereda and Feltre visited by road if desired.

On the other hand, those intending to see the route through should consider carrying adequate provisions and possibly bivouac gear too. Surface water is very scarce and will need to be carried quite extensively. As with the final stage of AV1, weigh up all factors carefully before setting out and endeavour to obtain a weather forecast.

From Passo Cereda, keep to the main road to just beyond Rifugio Padreterno and turn sharp R on a road through woods to the hamlet of

45 min - **MATTIUZZI** (1210m) - *possible lodging in private houses.*

From near a fountain, AV2 waymarks follow the road beyond the hamlet, taking a track off R (path 801) at a bend. Zig-zag up across

127

meadows and in forest, with impressive views ahead of Piz di Sagron. About 40 min up from Mattuizzi, a deep boulder-choked ravine is reached. Proceed along the L stony bank towards a narrow gap. In 1972 a massive landslip obliterated the path here and it was subsequently diverted, taking an extra 30-40 min. Recently, the original line has been restored across the debris and made secure by a long fixed rope. Great care is still needed in bad weather, especially after heavy storms when more loose material is prone to movement.

Beyond the landslip, AV2 continues on a marked path, skirting rock walls R and aiming at a high, narrow pass, reached up 200m of more difficult ground, including the traverse of a steep, slippery cliff. This leads out to an old smugglers' pass -

3½-4 hrs - **FORCELLA DI COMEDON** (2067m).

A short descent R (SW) negotiates a secondary saddle and a rough gully (possible frozen snow) down to the grassy Pian della Regina. A brief climb brings us to the buildings of

30 min - **BIVACCO FELTRE** (1930m) - *The corrugated-iron construction, though unsupervised, is well appointed for a bivouac hut, with 23 beds complete with mattresses and blankets, and a generous kitchen area with tables and chairs (but no stoves).*

Proceed W for a short distance to the lower of some water troughs (pure). The well-marked trail (801) drops S across the flowery Pian del Re and winds up steeper stony slopes beneath the contorted rock strata of Parete Piatta to Col dei Bechi (1960m). There are stunning views of the S wall of Sass de Mura, along the base of which AV2 finds its serpentine way on *Sentiero dei Caserin*.

This is difficult ground, exposed and aided in places where extra care is needed. Some large caves offer shelter in case of deteriorating weather and are interesting features. Before long, Caserin is reached and the going gets somewhat easier on grassy slopes to the Passo de Mura (1867m). In less than 1km, Passo Alvis is reached (good escape route L (E) on path 811 to Malgo Alvis and Val Canzoi), whereafter the route drops westwards to Malga Nevetta and

2½-3 hrs - **RIFUGIO BRUNO BOZ** (1718m) - *patronised almost exclusively by walkers on AV2! CAI Feltre section; 30 places; open end-June to end-Sept; tel; 0439/81738.*

(If necessary Val Noana can be reached on path 727, joining a stony

*Crossing a snow-filled gully below
Forcella di Comedon*

Lady's Slipper Orchid

track S.W.)

Despite the lush appearance of vegetation, surface water is scarce on the next section and it is wise to carry a good supply.

AV2 continues S up to the Monte Colsento ridge, then SW along it to Passo di Finestra (1766m), a depression between Monte Colsento and Monte Zoccare Alto. There is an electricity pylon nearby, an incongruous reminder of civilisation!

Watching out for waymarks, continue S for a few metres but then leave path 805 (which descends steeply SE to Val Canzoi) and zig-zag up R to just below the crest of Monte Zoccare Alto. Keeping under the ridge top, AV2 follows an artificial ledge cut into the rock (steel cable in places). The ridge itself is pierced by tunnels dating from World War 1 when these mountains, along with many others in the Dolomites, were the scene of fierce fighting between Austrian and Italian troops.

Sasso Scarnia (2226m) presents a wild and rugged prospect and our route zig-zags from a spur up steep steps cut into the rock itself. An aided stretch along the summit brings us out under the NE side at a broad shoulder, from which the path climbs beneath great cliffs, amongst huge boulders, before dropping across a gap and hugging the base of an overhang.

Now on the S slopes of Sasso Scarnia, proceed along past rock towers and gullies and interestingly jointed rock walls until eventually a track is met coming in from the L (from Forcella Scarnia). Having crossed an area of lilies and joined an old military mule-track. AV2 passes more rough ground and reaches a saddle SSW of Monte Ramezza.

(Here begins a permitted deviation from the path, signed at a

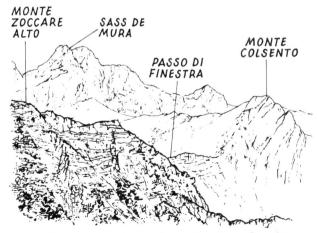

Retrospective view north-east from Sasso Scarnia

boulder L, to visit the *Busa de Giàzz*, a massive cave containing a cone of snow and ice, once used to supply the brewery at Pedavena and the town of Feltre with ice! Ice-axe, rope and crampons are needed for a full exploration of the cave. Allow 20 min each way to reach it and respect the Nature Reserve rules by keeping to the waymarked path).

AV2 continues, almost level, along the Costa Alpe Ramezza, then climbs R over the crest above, with a very exposed section on the N side high above the depths of Val Noana *(care needed)*. The trail turns S, traversing the uppermost perimeter of the boulder-strewn Piazza del Diavolo. The disorderly flow of huge stone blocks seems to have originated in a landslide; in any event, it is a most unusual place, the silence accentuating its unworldly appearance.

We are in a protected nature reserve, one of three in the Feltrini range and, linked with others farther north, the nucleus of a future Dolomites National Park. Anything which could alter or disturb the habitat is prohibited, including actions that could start a fire, leaving litter, rolling rocks, picking flowers, pulling up vegetation, hunting or alarming animals of any kind, collecting minerals or fossils, and bringing in dogs. There is great scientific interest in this area, especially amongst botanists, and such an ancient landscape, unaltered by human settlement, deserves very special consideration.

After crossing a steep rock face beneath Pietena (2195m), we come round on scree, past curiously formed stones reminiscent of ancient monuments, to the flat and grassy Passo di Pietena (2094m). The mule track winds down into a bowl of meadows surrounded by crags and scree and rich in flora. Near the sizeable mountain farm buildings is the only spring since Rifugio Bruno Boz.

Becoming level, the track leads on S, past a path junction R (817) to Monte Pavione, and climbs gently to the final high pass on AV2 -Passo le Vette Grande (1994m). From here, the panorama ahead is unequivocally a lowland one over the valley of the River Piave and the green pre-alps beyond. Just below the pass stands

5-6 hrs - **RIFUGIO GIORGIO DAL PIAZ** (1990m) - *CAI Feltre section; 34 places; open mid-June to mid-Sept; tel; 0439/9065.*

The old military road twists S, its bends short-cut for the walker. To the right is the green pyramid of Monte Pavione, at 2335m the highest point in the Feltrini Dolomites. Dropping through woods, we arrive at

1½ hrs - **PASSO DI CROCE D'AUNE** (1015m) - *buses for Pedavena.*

Leaving S, our route climbs and drops gently in woods along the N

Descending from Sasso Scarnia   133

slopes of Monte Avena on tracks to Rifugio Belvedere (967m) and thence by the *Sentiero dell' Armentera* down to

45 min - PEDAVENA (346m) - *hotels, inn, park, zoo! brewery! frequent bus services.*

On foot it is now just 3kms to the centre of

40 min - FELTRE (325m) - *CAI mountain rescue centre, hotels, restaurants, tourist office, railway station, coach services to Trento and Belluno, all supplies and services.*

Feltre is an unpretentious, very Italian town, notably less tourist-conscious than Belluno, its counterpart on AV1. The old town, still surrounded by walls and dominated by its castle in an enclave of Renaissance architecture, has been destroyed and rebuilt many times in its chequered history. There are old churches, a civic museum with paintings and sculptures, a theatre, a University Institute of modern languages and the fascinating *Galleria Carlo Rizzarda* dedicated to wrought-iron work.

A visit to the tourist office to enter names in the AV2 register will be rewarded with souvenir badges and a chance to contemplate on the long, high mountain route stretching back in time and distance to Bressanone and the Plose summit where it all began.

*An old club Alpina Italiano signboard
at Feltre*

135

GLOSSARY

ACQUA - water

ALBERGO - hotel

ALPINISTICO - for climbers

ALTA VIA - high level mountain route with few technical difficulties

ALTIPIANO - high tableland

BIVACCO - bivouac hut (no guardian but basic equipment)

CAMPANILE - rock spire (literally 'church steeple')

CAMPEGGIO - camping

CARTA GEOGRAFICA - map

CASERA - small mountain hut of wood or stone

CIMA - mountain summit

COL - mountain summit, usually subsidiary

EST or ORIENTE - east

FIUME - river

FORCELLA (FORC) - narrow saddle between higher ground

FUNIVIA - cable-car

GHIACCIAIO - glacier

GRANDE - large

GRUPPO - mountain group

LAGO - lake

MALGA - mountain farm (if occupied may provide dairy foods)

MEZZO - middle

MONTE - mountain

NORD or SETTENTRIONE - north

NUOVA PERCORSO - new routing

OVEST or OCCIDENTE - west

PASSO - mountain pass or saddle

PIAN - stretch of level ground

PICCOLO - small

PONTE - bridge

PORTA - small mountain pass

PREVISIONI DE TEMPO - weather forecast

PUNTA - mountain peak

RECAPITO POSTALE - postal address

RIFUGIO - mountain refuge

ROTABILE - road

SASSO - rocky peak

SCARPONE DA MONTAGNE -hiking boot

SEGGIOVA - chair lift

SENTIERO - path

SUD or MERIDIONE - south

TAPPA - stage or leg (in a journey)

TELEFONO - telephone

TORRE - tower

VAL/VALLE - valley

VIA FERRATA - mountain route, often steep and exposed but provided with metal cables, rungs and ladders as climbing aids and protection

VIA NORMALE - normal ascent route

HEIGHT CONVERSION TABLE

Metres	Feet	Metres	Feet
500	1639	1800	5903
600	1967	1900	6231
700	2295	2000	6559
800	2623	2100	6887
900	2951	2200	7215
1000	3279	2300	7543
1100	3607	2400	7871
1200	3935	2500	8199
1300	4263	2600	8527
1400	4591	2700	8855
1500	4919	2800	9183
1600	5247	2900	9511
1700	5575	3000	9839

SUMMARY TABLE OF ROUTES AND PRINCIPAL VARIANTS

(Timings shown are maximum, given normal conditions)

ALTA VIA 1

STAGE 1

Lago di Braies			2h	- Rifugios Fanes & Varella
2h 45m	- Porta Sora 'l Forn		1h	- Malga Fanes Grande
10m	- Rifugio Biella		1h 45m	- Forcella del Lago
45m	- Rifugio Sennes		1h 45m	- Rifugio Monte Lagazuoi
1h	- Rifugio Pederü			

STAGE 2

30m	- Forcella Col dei Bos		1h	- Forcella Staulanza
30m	- Bar Magistrato		1h	- Casere di Piòda
1h 15m	- Path junction with variant*		1h 15m	- Rifugio Coldai
45m	- Rifugio Nuvolau		1h 45m	- Forcella di Col Reàn
1h	- Passo Giau		1h 40m	- Rifugio Vazzoler
1h	- Forcella Giau		1h 30m	- Forcella Col dell'Orso
1h 15m	- Forcella Ambrizzola		1h 15m	- Rifugio Carestiato
1h	- Forcella Roan		30m	- Passo Duran
30m	- Rifugio Citta di Fiume			

*Variant from path junction

20m	- Rifugio Cinque Torri
2h	- Lago & Rifugio Federa
50m	- Forcella Ambrizzola

STAGE 3

20m	- Forcella Dagarei		1h 10m	- Casera Nerville
3h	- Forcella Moschesin		2h	- Forcella del Marmol
1h	- Rifugio Pramperet		15m	- Bivacco Bocco
2h	- Forcella Sud del Van de Citta		3h	- Rifugio 7 Alpini
1h	- Bivacco Renzo del Mas		2h	- Case Bortot
1h	- Forcella La Varetta		2h	- Belluno

138

ALTA VIA 2

STAGE 1

Bressanone

1h	- San Andrea
5h	- Rifugio Plose
1h 25m	- Sporthotel
55m	- Passo Rodella
2h	- Forcella della Putia
30m	- Rifugio Genova
40m	- Path junction with variant*

2h	- Forcella della Roa
1n	- Forcella Forces de Sielles
1h 30m	- Rifugio Puez
1h 45m	- Passo di Crespeina
1h	- Passo Gardena

*Variant from path junction
1h 30m - Forcella Pana
45m   - Rifugio Firenze
1h 30m - Forcella Forces de Sielles

STAGE 2

2h 15m	- Rifugio Pissadü
3h 30m	- Rifugio Boè
1h 45m	- Passo Pordoi
1h	- Rifugio Vial del Pan
50m	- Rifugio Castiglioni*
1h 30m	- Malga Ciapela
3h	- Passo di Forca Rossa
1h 45m	- Passo di San Pellegrino

*Marmolada variant
from Rifugio Castiglioni

2h 30m	- Rifugio Pian dei Fiacconi
3h 30m	- Forcella della Marmolada
1h 30m	- Rifugio Contrin
2h	- Passo Cirelle
1h 45m	- Passo di San Pellegrino

STAGE 3

3h	- Passo di Valles
1h	- Passo di Venegiotta
4h	- Rifugio Mulaz
1h 30m	- Passo delle Farangole
3h	- Rifugio Pedrotti
2h 30m	- Rifugio Pradidali

1h 30m	- Passo delle Lede
45m	- Bivacco Minazio
1h 30m	- Rifugio Treviso
2h	- Forcella d'Oltro
2h 30	- Passo Cereda

STAGE 4

45m	- Mattiuzzi	5-6h	- Rifugo Giorgio dal Piaz
4h	- Forcella di Comedon	1h 30m	- Passo di Croce d'Aune
30m	- Bivacco Feltre	45m	- Pedavena
3h	- Rifugio Bruno Boz	40m	- Feltre

SPACE FOR REFUGE RUBBER STAMPS

Printed by Carnmor Print & Design, 95/97, London Road, Preston, Lancashire.

The Sella group from above Passo Gardena